The Learning School

Ruth Sutton

with illustrations by Jim Whittaker

RS Publications

Published by RS Publications
29 Nevile Court, Nevile Road,
Salford M7 3PS, England, UK
Telephone & Fax +44 (0)161 708 8880

Printed and bound in Great Britain by
John Roberts & Sons Printers (Salford) Ltd
Chapel Street, Salford

ISBN 0 9523871 2 3

Acknowledgements

Once again, in this latest book in the series, the same people have made the same contributions as before. I wrote the text, Jim Whittaker drew the cartoons, and Mary McSherry pulled it all together, guiding the book through to the printers, and then on into schools on four continents. Thanks are due also to Lynn Jeary for her help with desktop publishing advice and to Katherine Toye for her editorial advice.

I am as ever grateful to all the teachers, school managers, administrators, teacher educators, researchers and others who have shared their experience and ideas with me over many years. All I do is listen, think, and offer them back in a form which will hopefully help schools make a difference.

Contents

Contents

Introduction

Several years ago I wrote a book entitled 'Assessment: a Framework for Teachers'. I wanted to explore and 'de-mystify' an aspect of teaching which had such rich potential for improving both learning and teaching but seemed to worry teachers and to be associated almost entirely with external tests and examinations. The book was concise, jargon-free, full of examples recognisable to teachers, and designed to motivate those who read it to think and read more. It sold well and seemed to achieve what I had hoped for.

Further books followed, based on the same design–one on 'School Self Review' (1994) and the next, 'Assessment for Learning' (1995), aimed to build on the earlier assessment book and pursue some specific issues and ideas which have emerged in recent years as worthy of closer scrutiny. This book included chapters on 'Planning', 'Involving Students', 'Standards and Standardising' and 'Portfolios'.

'The Learning School' is prompted by three needs which have been turning in my head and may now be ready to be tackled. The first is my continuing interest in the dilemma at the heart of all educational assessment. This dilemma was the basis of the first chapter in 'Assessment: a Framework for Teachers' in 1991 and will be the first focus in Chapter One here too, thought through with the benefit of six eventful years experience. This experience has generated Chapters Two and Three which deal respectively with 'Feedback' and 'Feedforward and Target-setting'. 'Weighing the baby doesn't make it grow' goes the old saying, and these two chapters are devoted to what we do with assessment data when we have it.

My second motive is to begin from the premise that teachers are learners too, and to apply what we know about effective assessment to the 'appraisal' of teachers. Many educational systems round the world are currently interested in 'measuring' the effectiveness of teachers, for a variety of reasons, and so am I. The area is fraught with difficulties both technical and political: my aim is to apply to it the same principles of sound assessment for learning, in the hope of generating some light on a possible way forward.

The third need underpinning this book is to make connections between the three contexts of assessment: the assessment of students, the evaluation of the school's development, and the appraisal of the teachers. The same assessment principles underpin these three, and all of them have at their heart an investigation into the quality of learning. Much of the information we need to check for all three is found in the classroom – and there is no place more important for educators to focus their attention.

Hence the structure of the book: the first three chapters deal with the principles and impact of effective assessment, using for illustration the relatively familiar context of the assessment of students' learning. The subsequent chapters apply these principles to the 'assessment' of the whole school and its teachers. The final chapter makes the connections between these three contexts and draws some conclusions about how schools under pressure can achieve the maximum return from the investment of the intelligence and commitment of all those who work in them.

Before moving on, however, another of the book's intentions needs to be presented. The issues addressed here are not unique to one country or one phase of the education service, although the ways in which they manifest themselves are affected by assumptions based on language, culture, and history. I want to acknowledge both the similarities and the differences which exist in the daily lives of the teachers I work with, in the United Kingdom, New Zealand, Canada, the USA and South Africa. Some of the similarities have become especially noticeable over the past decade, stemming from a cluster of political views about education born in 'Thatcher's Britain' and since exported, along with other political imperatives about the efficacy of the 'free market' to solve public as well as private sector problems.

The 'New Right' and its policies continue to have a profound effect on education in many of the countries I work in. The election of the British Labour Party to government in May 1997 marks a turning point, and the rejection of the 'free market' as the underpinning principle, but many of the previous emphases remain in place. Part of legacy is the use of assessment as the means whereby the 'output' of the education service can be 'quantified' for two main purposes. Firstly, 'output data' can be used to promote competition between schools, which is assumed to raise standards. Secondly, statistical information will be offered to 'consumers' (parents) to enable them to make sound choices among 'providers' (schools). Add a 'price tag' to each student enrolled by the school and the market-driven picture is complete. Complete but flawed. More detail is needed here to make sense of some of the assumptions, strategies and contradictions we can identify, and to understand the special role played by assessment – of students, of teachers, and of schools.

Preface:
The Global Context of 'New Right' Education Policy

What follows is an attempt to explain fairly simply a political development of great complexity, and the source of much contention. I present the beliefs on which 'New Right' policy is based as objectively as I can. I do not agree with many of these beliefs, but their existence is undeniable, and they do help to explain the multi-faceted nature of the policies which follow, including the central role played by assessment procedures. If political debate bores or irritates you, skip to the beginning of Chapter One, and return to this section later if you need to.

At the heart of this set of ideas is a belief in 'less government', and faith in the operation of a free market to regulate society and maximise productivity. In pursuit of less government, the public sector should be privatised wherever possible, and central taxation reduced to the minimum necessary to maintain the few central services which remain.

In order for the market to operate efficiently in the field of education, it will be necessary in the early stages for central government to be quite interventionist, in order to clear away any potential barriers to the freedom of the market. Such barriers could include intermediate structures, such as local education authorities or school boards, which lie between the central government and the local providers and consumers. A further barrier will, it is assumed, be the entrenched self-protection and resistance to change of those with a vested interest in the status quo, for example teachers' trade unions and professional associations. The public sector services of health and education are considered particularly vulnerable to 'professionalism', which is assumed to mean that they invest energy in protecting themselves from 'non-professionals' and anything else which could undermine their status. These attitudes will need to be attacked with vigour if their retrograde influence is to be successfully combated. In health and education therefore the needs of the 'consumers' (patients and parents) will be contrasted with the needs of the providers (doctors and other health professionals, teachers and other education professionals), and consumers' needs must be given precedence.

From these simple, not to say simplistic, and powerful premises, a range of educational priorities emerge for any 'New Right' government. The order in which they are tackled may vary from country to country, but the components remain clearly recognisable.

1. **Responsibility for educational provision is apparently shifted from the centre to the locality,** although actual control remains centralised. In small systems like New Zealand. This was accomplished at a stroke with the dissolution of all regional management structures and the establishment of a Board of Trustees for each of the 2,700 schools. In the United Kingdom, the attack on Local Education Authorities has been unremitting but as yet unsuccessful, although many of the larger LEAs have been split into smaller units whose future viability is as yet uncertain. In Ontario, the break up of school boards has just begun. Once these structures have been dissolved, it is extremely difficult to re-establish them if the new procedures turn out to be unsuccessful.

Schools are placed largely under local management, with 'boards' representing parents and the local community. These boards may hire and fire teachers, look after the buildings, monitor the school's budget and development, but their powers are clearly limited. None of the 'New Right' systems, for example, have allowed the local boards to determine more than a small proportion of the curriculum to be taught. The curriculum is designed centrally, with as little involvement of teachers as is practicable, in case the teachers substitute their needs for those of the parents or the state, who between them pick up most of the bills and should therefore have the most say.

One of the inherent problems in this model is a continuing disagreement, within the 'New Right' itself, about what the centrally designed curriculum should aim for. Those looking to a future of technology, global competition and the unforeseen expansion of knowledge will want a curriculum which encourages new ways of working, flexibility, problem-solving, and sophisticated computer skills. Those nostalgic for a past uncontaminated by 'welfarism', 'big government', 'isms', and 'ologies' will favour more traditional content and methods. The tension between these two visions of the future surfaces in ambivalence about priorities and some uneasy compromises. In England and Wales in the 1980's, for example, the Department of Employment was supporting the Technical and Vocational Education Initiative (TVEI) for 14-18 year olds which emphasised learning to learn, problem solving, and relevance to the world of work in both the content and methods of teaching. Simultaneously the Department of Education proposed a National Curriculum arranged in traditional subject areas, which bore little or no resemblance to the goals of TVEI.

2. A continuing and simultaneous theme, already hinted at, is **distrust of professional associations and unions, their concerns and their influence on policy.** A dark picture is painted of a past in which teachers and policy makers, both local and national, colluded with each other and ignored the needs and entitlements of parents and students alike. Collusion over policy extended into non-existent or flabby accountability systems. None of this could continue. Policy

would therefore be made without consultation with bodies representing education professionals. Even educational research as the basis of policy is suspect because it is produced by those very educational 'experts' who have allowed the quality of public education to decline.

The view that teachers are more interested in protecting themselves than meeting the needs of the students is deeply felt in some circles, however unfair or unproven we may consider it to be. It has a crucial bearing on assessment policy as it leads to a lack of faith in teachers' ability to assess their students fairly and honestly, which in turn affects the structure of national assessment procedures. It has a bearing too on the ways in which teachers are trained, inducted into the profession, periodically checked to ensure the quality of their efforts, rewarded (or not) and offered continuing professional development. Should the appraisal of teachers be linked to pay? Who should make a judgement about teacher quality, and against whose definitions and standards? All these are assessment questions – brought into sharp focus by the current interest in 'evidence' and 'results' – for teachers and schools as well as students.

To ensure that teachers and schools follow the legal requirements and do not subvert them in practice, a rigorous form of school 'inspection' forms a further strand of the package of policies. Such inspection will have two main purposes: first to check compliance with the law, and second to gather and publish evidence of the quality of school 'outputs' so that parents are able to make good consumer choices between schools. External 'disinterested' (i.e. neutral) inspectors will be used, and detailed reports published. Successful schools will be more popular with consumers, and therefore rewarded with greater student numbers and more money, while unsuccessful schools will be revealed in all their inadequacy by the searchlight of external scrutiny. Parents making sensible choices will

decide against them, and thus deprived of 'customers' the school will eventually 'cease trading'. Raw competition will produce winners and losers and the losers will go out of business by this 'natural' process, relieving both central and local government of difficult decisions about the future of 'failing' schools.

This deceptively simple idea produces some agonising implications about the rights of a community and its citizens to a high-quality local publicly-funded school. Through the untrammelled operation of such a system, some communities, often in areas of socio-economic deprivation, find themselves further deprived as a result of the collapse of the local school, and the disparities of education provision get wider before, presumably, they rectify themselves through the continuing 'natural' influence of the market. But what if the 'natural' influence of the market does not work, or takes too long? In the meantime the one chance of a quality education for some students is at risk. Intervention or non-intervention – that is the question: there is mounting evidence that, whatever the theory, politicians faced with the reactions of voters to the collapse of parts of the public education service often use public money to keep failing schools afloat – a laudable move, but inconsistent with the basic tenets of their own policy.

3. The third main piece in this ill-fitting jigsaw involves **assessment to produce quantifiable 'results'**: there seems to be minimal patience for any educational 'outputs' which cannot be expressed in numerical form. Words, it is argued, are notoriously subjective and unhelpful for drawing up 'league tables' or for statistical analysis.

   The key purpose of assessment in this new climate is to provide the market with reliable information on which to base educational choices and decisions. Assessment strategies will check 'outputs' relative to the required 'inputs' of the state's curriculum requirements. A tension has to be resolved between the need for 'measurement' and the characteristics of some of the inputs. In the debate between those who look to the future to provide the state curriculum and those who look to the past, the latter have a great advantage as their preferred curriculum seems much easier to assess, with its plethora of facts and certainties and the emphasis clearly on memory and regurgitation rather than problem-solving methods which are notoriously problematic for assessment designers.

   The expression of these desired curriculum outputs in terms of pre-described 'levels' or 'standards' provides a number to indicate achievement, and these numbers can then be de-coded to explain what students are judged to have learned. Decisions have to be made about the number of levels, and whether to adopt one set of levels for the whole of schooling or one set per stage. England and Wales decided initially on 10 levels, which seemed neat and intelligible, to be assessed periodically between the ages of 5 and 16. However technical difficulties of the relationship between levels and grades in existing public examinations finally reduced the number of levels to 8 (plus a 9th for 'exceptional performance') and the assessment events to students aged 7, 11 and 14. In New Zealand there are 8 levels within the National Curriculum, and another tricky interface between these levels and the next set used for the Qualifications Framework. South Africa has largely followed the New Zealand model, and in Ontario the decision was for 4 levels in each band of years.

The drive for quantification is not necessarily a problem for assessment, so long as we recognise the limitations of the information thus generated, but the use of numbers can add a veneer of apparent objectivity to what is still a complex process of human judgement. It encourages a climate of impatience with the immeasurable, even though some of the most fundamental 'outputs' of education are the hardest to measure. How can a number be used to describe a young person's preparedness for adult life, or a child's willingness to take risks to extend her learning, or tolerance of the views of one's peers, or acceptance of personal responsibility?

Many English-speaking cultures have a respect for numbers and a tendency to disrespect that which cannot be measured. In this cultural climate, the best we can do to provide a balanced view of the outcomes of learning is to pursue 'multiple measures' and 'triangulate' them to find an approximation of reality, which is more expensive, complex and time-consuming than policy makers hoped for.

No doubt many a Minister of Education or her/his equivalent has heartily wished that the resolution of these tensions would be easier than it turns out to be. No doubt, also, many a teacher has yearned for the opportunity to get on and do the job without the unnecessary intrusion of such overtly political ambitions into the policies which determine many of their daily activities in the school. Unfortunately for them both, over the past few years the post-war consensus about education in the democratic state has been challenged, as has the role played by assessment. In these circumstances it is more than ever necessary to review current developments in assessment against some fundamental principles, both to analyse what is happening and to suggest a way ahead.

Chapter One:
The Framework of Ideas

Learning is not an extra dimension in our lives: it is integral to the human condition. As babies we learn the spoken language, a task of staggering complexity, by observing and listening, mimicry and analysis of the structure of both words and sentences. Many children learn to read the same way, with or without specific prompting from parents and teachers. We learn by absorbing information from all around us, connecting it with what we already know, trying new ideas and new skills and getting feedback. Sometimes the learning is by 'trial and error', and the learner alone has to work out what went well and what went wrong, and why, and what to do next. Some learners are very persistent, others give up more easily. Sometimes feedback is provided for us by someone else, whose job it is to tell us what went well and what went wrong, and what to do next. Sometimes we get a different kind of help – from someone who encourages us to think about what we're learning, but helps by asking questions rather than providing all the answers.

In all these cases, assessment is going on. Information is gathered about what's been learned, and conclusions are derived from this information. It's an integral part of both learning and teaching. This chapter is about the Three Big Ideas which need to be understood to make sense of the assessment process, and to help us make good choices about it. Here are the Three Big Ideas:

1. Assessment is integral to teaching and learning

2. Five Key Questions have to be answered, starting with Why?

3. A 'best fit' must be found between validity, reliability, manageability/cost, and public acceptability.

Big Idea Number 1

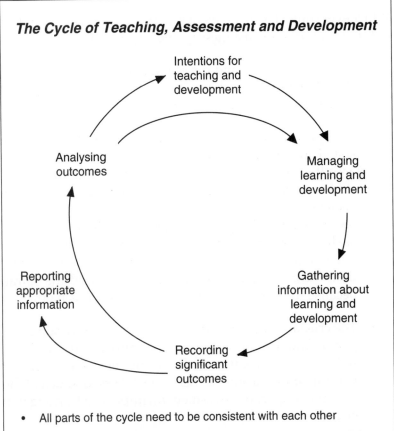

The Cycle of Teaching, Assessment and Development

Intentions for teaching and development

Managing learning and development

Gathering information about learning and development

Recording significant outcomes

Reporting appropriate information

Analysing outcomes

- All parts of the cycle need to be consistent with each other
- The cycle is complete only when information is 'fed forward' into planning and management of learning
- 'Assessment' described here as 'observing the outcomes of learning' is integral to teaching
- Assesment promotes learning through specific feedback to the learner

This diagram could represent the learning of an individual student, or a group, or a whole cohort, and the learners could be young or old – child or teacher. It could even represent the school itself, with the school's 'intentions' expressed in the school's development plan.

Whichever context of assessment we are interested in, the nature of this spiral brings some inescapable implications.

- Plans for learning and development must be sufficiently flexible to respond to the unexpected as well as the expected outcomes of previous learning.

- Each part of this spiral is connected to every other part. The stated intentions for learning should be reflected in the activities we design to support these intentions; the information we gather should relate closely to the achievement of our original intentions; the written or other records we keep should also relate to our original intentions, as should the reports through which we communicate with others about achievement. If any part of this cycle is changed, the reverberations should be felt right round the spiral, because the parts cannot be sealed off from each other.

- The crucial stage which turns this process into a spiral not just a straight line is the one concerned with analysis, reflection and 'feedforward' into the next intentions for teaching and learning. If this stage is missed, much of the potential impact of assessment on improved learning will be lost.

- If you're not clear and specific about what you're trying to achieve, the assessment task becomes extremely difficult, because you're not sure where to look to find the information.

Can you think of any further implications which follow from this very basic representation of the teaching and learning cycle?

Big Idea Number 2

Effective assessment requires us to consider five Key Questions as we design assessment strategies. These questions are:

Why? ...What's the purpose, and who is it for?

What? ...do we look for to check that learning has happened?

Who? ...is the most appropriate person to find the information?

How? ...What's the most appropriate method to use?

So What? ...What do we do with the information when we have it?

Question 1: Why?

'Fitness for purpose' could be called the Golden Rule of assessment. A wide range of purposes can be pursued through assessment, and the first choice is to be clear which one, or more than one, we are interested in. Until you're clear on this, you can go no further, so let's take the possible purposes one at a time and exemplify them. These purposes are not better or worse than each other, they're just different so the order is not significant.

- Assessment for specific information, about learning and teaching, in relation to specific 'criteria', ie expected outcomes and standards.

  A school may discuss and decide the expectations for high-quality classroom teaching, and teachers are then assessed to check that they are achieving these expectations, and to what degree or standard.

- Assessment to demonstrate an individual's progress over time, compared to his/her own previous best.

  The teacher will check each student's work against his/her previous best, and assess the extent of the student's progress,

15

> *judging whether the progress is acceptable for that student, within the time frame. The criteria and the standard expected may be particular to the individual student.*

- Assessment to compare one learner's achievement with the achievements of the other learners, to discover an 'order of merit'. This form of assessment is not designed to discover what learners have actually learned or not learned, but only to distinguish learners from each other.

  > *Teachers were to be rewarded for 'excellence' but as the reward was financial, and only a limited amount of money was available for this purpose, only a certain number of teachers could gain such a reward, regardless of how many had achieved the required standard of 'excellence in teaching'. The assessment of the teachers therefore meant that they were competing against each other for the award rather than against the expected standards.*

These differences of purpose fundamentally affect the design of the assessment. Distinctions are often made in terms of the 'referencing' of the assessment, meaning the basis of the judgement being made. Criterion or standards-referencing is one approach; norm-referencing is another; self or ipsative-referencing is a third (from the Latin *ipse* meaning *self*). To make life really confusing for those receiving information about assessment, we sometimes use codes to summarise performance, such as letter grades or numbers. When we give the learner a 'B' grade, does this mean a 'B' in relation to the rest of the group (or the national cohort), a 'B' in relation to the specific learning expectations defined as worthy of a 'B', or does it mean that the learner has gained a 'B' in relation to his/her own previous best performance. Even if the teacher is clear what the 'B' actually means, the student or the parent may not be. Moreover, if the purpose of the report was to improve the student's performance, how does information in this form help to achieve that?

Problems arise when the same assessment process is used to meet a number of purposes which may be hard to reconcile with each other. Meeting them all simultaneously is an attractive proposition because it may look more efficient, cheaper or more manageable, but in trying to achieve multiple purposes we could end up achieving none of them satisfactorily. The advantages and disadvantages have sometimes to be carefully weighed against each other to find the best solution in the circumstances.

So, purpose is crucial. So is audience – who the assessment is for. If we intend to use assessment information to communicate with someone, then in the true spirit of effective communication we have to consider how to represent the information so that it can be properly understood by its intended audience. Even if the information is useful it has to be communicated in such a way that it can be used.

Educators are professional communicators, so we should be really good at this, but are we? Is poor communication about the outcomes of assessment a problem of skill, or will? Or is it often the result of more compromises, between the quality of communication and the time it takes to produce it, for example.

> *We know that 'marking/grading' a student's work while sitting alongside her and talking about it as we go will have a greater impact on future learning than taking the work away and returning it later, relying on codes or written remarks to offer guidance about future learning. We know it, but we teach 150 students every week and have to meet certain expectations about the amount of written work to be set for them. Maybe the only way through is to plan to 'mark' with each student we teach at least once a semester, or once a month, whatever we feel we can manage.*

> *We know too that parents have traditionally expected a written report about their child's learning and progress once every nine weeks, or three times a year, or whatever the established practice has been. But the type of information we are now assessing has changed, as the curriculum requirements of the province or state have changed, to incorporate more specific learning standards expressed in words. We could write these more lengthy and specific reports with the same frequency as before, but the time we spend doing that we cannot spend doing anything else, such as preparing useful resources, sharing ideas with colleagues or even talking to the students themselves. Something has to give.*

Purpose and audience will be our guide, but the choices are rarely easy.

Question 2: What? ...do we look for to check that learning has happened?

Idea No 1, about the place of assessment as part of the teaching and learning cycle, has already offered some guidance on this question. What we look for in the assessment process will be the expected outcomes of our teaching intentions. Assessment, after all, is about gathering evidence and making a judgement. If our teaching intentions are very specific, then we should have little difficulty deciding what to assess, although we may have a problem with the sheer quantity of information we have to gather. If, on the other hand, we are not very specific about what we aim to teach, the choice of assessment criteria is problematic. We may be left just looking at everything the learner can show us, trying to decide what it really signifies.

To put the problem in a nutshell: tight teaching objectives may be good for assessment but not so good for teaching; loose teaching objectives may be good for teaching but not so good for assessment.

There was a time in teaching when teachers and schools had more freedom of choice about what to teach than they have now, except for those teachers and students facing clear high-stake expectations in external examination syllabuses or 'prescriptions'. For the systems I work in – the UK, New Zealand, South Africa, some Canadian provinces, and states of the US – that time has passed and shows no sign of returning. Required curriculums are now the order of the day – for reasons I have tried to explain in the Preface of this book. Some of these required curriculums are both specific and 'crowded': not much room for flexibility or leaving the space for response to unanticipated learning needs. This means that there's little ambiguity about the assessment criteria, but there are far too many of them to do a really good job. The choice faced currently by these teachers is the choice of what to assess when, to avoid if possible an unmanageable and unsatisfactory overload of assessment activity. These external

Teacher's Planning: the Loose/Tight Dilemma

Tight

Positive Impact

Absolutely clear expecations, scripted to perfection, very detailed resource planning possible. Teacher and students know exactly where they stand. Required coverage guaranteed.

Able to pursue the anticipated learning needs of specific students. 'Constructivist' student-centred

Negative Impact

No opportunity to respond to unanticpated learning need. The needs of the plan override anything else. Students have no 'voice'

Aimless, no chance for detailed forward planning. No guarantee of covering required curriculum

Loose

Remember
Learning not 'coverage'.
Build in time for

- the unexpected
- Remediation, consolidation, extension
- review and target-setting

---

pressures may drive teachers to pursue large amounts of assessment, but quantity may adversely affect both the quality of the assessment data, and the teachers' response to it.

The implications for planning what is to be taught are also tricky, and I've written at greater length about this elsewhere (Assessment for Learning, 1995, Chapter One). Suffice to say that planning has to find a balance between 'loose' and 'tight', probably by making teaching intentions more focussed than before, but leaving space within every plan for response to the unexpected, or to the spontaneous 'teachable moment' which can have such a positive impact on teachers and learners alike, or to enable periodic review and target-setting as part of the natural course of events.

The specificity and quantity of teaching intentions will be the starting point for finding the 'What?' of the assessment process. As I have suggested elsewhere, one way through is to start your planning with the 'big picture' expectation over a year or longer, work out your priorities in terms of what will be taught and assessed over the longest span of time you can practically envisage, and then plan backwards to decide what will be the particular focus of each 'chunk' of teaching and learning along the way. Selecting key objectives for both teaching and assessment will help you to then plan with greater care by avoiding overload.

A small number of assessment criteria, a carefully planned assessment strategy, and purposeful use of the information to achieve the desired impact is far more valuable than lots of poor information which you have neither the time nor the inclination to use. **Our assessment strategies need to emphasise quality rather than quantity.**

> *A team of teachers were planning together a 'topic' of work for their students on 'Tadpoles'. They began by 'mapping' all the various learning activities they could use, and listing all the learning which could possibly be achieved through a study of tadpoles. The list of learning activities and possibilities was impressive, ranging from writing*

about the life cycle of the frog, through working with others to monitor the development of the frogspawn and on into grasping and articulating an understanding of metamorphosis. If the teachers were to assess all these possible learning outcomes they would have to make it manageable by assessing everything as quickly and simply as they could. They could give the students a quick multi-choice test to check their knowledge of certain terminology, and ask them to label a diagram about the life cycle of the frog, but checking real understanding of metamorphosis was more difficult. One way to do so, they decided, would be to have a conversation with each student individually, asking open-ended questions which required the student to think, make connections, and explain metamorphosis using examples from a number of creatures as well as frogs. But this would have taken too long, so they settled instead for a group assignment to produce a wall display about metamorphosis. They were not convinced that this would really provide them with the evidence of individual students' understanding, but it was the best they could manage. When challenged about the choice they had made, they agreed that they had taken the easy way out, and compromised by removing 'understanding of metamorphosis' from their list of expected outcomes.

Do you recognise this dilemma? What other choices did these teachers have?

Another team of teachers were working on guidelines for classroom observation as part of the teacher appraisal process in their school. For a while they focussed on the mechanics — where the observer should be in the classroom, how long they should stay, and so on — and then realised that they would have to go back to deciding what they meant by 'the quality of teaching' and what 'indicators' of this quality would be visible to an observer in the classroom. Until they were clear about this they couldn't make sensible decisions about the methods employed to find these indicators. They had tried to skip the 'What' question, but had to go back to it before they could go on. Then I encouraged them to go back even further and consider first what was the purpose of the teacher appraisal process of which classroom observation was a part, and who was it for, and they began to consider how evidence of the quality of teaching might be found not only in the classroom but also in the perceptions of the students about their learning. When they got stuck on the 'What' one way out was to go back and remember the 'Why?' Then they had to go on to consider who should observe in the classroom and check the perceptions of the students, and how both could be managed without impossible demands on time and resources.

Assessment criteria – the 'what' of the assessment process – are a specific expression of expected outcomes. These outcomes provide us with assessment opportunities, from which we have to choose: trying to assess everything would force us into doing too much too fast. If choice is inevitable, we might be tempted to choose those outcomes which would be the easiest to identify, but this might not properly represent the balance of our intentions. We have to choose assessment criteria with care, and bear in mind that **the most visible evidence of learning may not be the most valuable, and the most manageable may not be the most meaningful.** Here's a dilemma if ever I saw one, definitely worth exploring further, as we decide **who** should gather assessment information, and **how**.

Question 3: Who?...is the most appropriate person to find the information?

Whether we are assessing students' learning, teachers' teaching, or the school's development, we always have a range of people to choose from when deciding who would be the best person or persons to check the answer to the 'What' question.

At one end of the continuum of choice would be someone quite external to the process, who does not know the person or the school being assessed, but who does have expertise in the area being checked. Such an 'outside' person may be more 'disinterested' (that is, neutral) and therefore less likely to have any preconceptions about the performance they are being asked to assess. On the other hand, the outsider may not understand all the nuances of the performance and may therefore miss some important evidence.

At the other end of the continuum would be the person or team being assessed, who knows more about themselves than anyone else could, and may therefore be best placed to make an accurate judgement. The student herself may know that she doesn't really understand something and is merely regurgitating what she has learned by heart, even though this may not be apparent to the assessor. The teacher or the school may know that they have put on a special show when the school inspectors are in school, which will stop as soon as they have departed, none the wiser. Self-assessment can be the most appropriate method in some circumstances, when the person being assessed has information less easily available to anyone else. It has potential problems also, however. The student may not be expert enough in the area being assessed to know how well he or she really understands it. The teacher may know full well that their performance is not typical, but may want to leave a favourable impression if future career opportunities will be affected by the assessment being made. Self-interest and absolute honesty do not always go hand in hand.

Between these two extremes are a variety of intermediaries who are expert enough in both the person being assessed and the focus of the assessment to make a good judgement. The class teacher is such a person in the assessment of a student's learning, or the teacher's 'critical friend' in the appraisal process – willing and able to give useful feedback as a fellow professional, and interested in the students' needs as well as the teacher's.

Depending on the purpose of the assessment , and considering what we are actually looking for in the assessment process, we make the best choice we can from the people available to us.

Traditionally, the more 'high stake' the assessment, the more external the assessor. One can understand why. High stake assessment has to be seen to be fair, and to avoid the ethical dilemmas which might result from expecting people to be absolutely impartial and honest when they have much to gain or lose from the judgements being made. The price of this tradition, however, is that the judgement may not be accurate , as it cannot take account of the circumstances surrounding the assessment, or may focus too much on evidence easily visible to an outsider. The observer of a teacher at work in the classroom may mistake good classroom control for teaching which is positively extending students' learning. The external examiner may find it difficult to assess a student's true grasp of something if he is unfamiliar with the student's style of expressing himself.

Question 4: How? ... What's the most appropriate method to use?

Here again, in any assessment context, there are a range of methods to choose from, and the assessment designer's task is to make the best choice, depending on the agreed purpose and criteria. In assessing student's learning we could:

- ask the student oral questions, and listen to the oral response, in the language of instruction, or in the student's own first language;

- give the student written questions, and read the written response, in the language of instruction, or in the student's own first language;

- watch the student over a period of time under normal classroom conditions;

25

- watch the student on a particular occasion under 'test conditions';

- give the student an assignment to be completed by a given deadline and meeting certain criteria;

- give the student the questions in advance to prepare answers which have to be presented on a specific occasion without support materials, or with support materials but within a tight timeframe;

- use a multi-choice test, a short answer test, an essay test;

- give an assignment to a group of students and assess the group's performance;

- use a range of types of evidence, demonstrated over a long period, and come to a considered overall judgement.

These are a few examples of the possibilities of methods available to us. They involve decisions about how we tell the students what we want them to show us, and decisions about the 'mode of response' – oral, written or practical, closed or open time, with or without access to books or calculators, individually or as part of a group, and so on.

Some of the choices we make about methods when designing assessment are logistical or technical. Other choices, however, can involve assumptions about ways of working, learning and demonstrating learning which are deeply significant culturally. English-speaking or European systems may set great store on learning being demonstrated quickly, or by the individual without collaboration with others, but these are choices made based on values we may not examine very often, and which are by no means universal. Why do we insist that learning should be demonstrated within very tight timeframes? Why do we insist that learners have to be assessed individually, and that collaboration is now regarded as cheating? What are the consequences of these choices for including or excluding certain ways of demonstrating learning?

> *One of the fascinations of assessment as an issue in education is the speed of transition from apparently easy technical questions to hard philosphical ones.*
>
> *Question: 'What's the best format for my record book?'*
> *Answer: 'It depends what you want to record.'*
>
> *Question: 'What information will I need to keep track of?'*
> *Answer: 'It depends what you're trying to teach.'*
>
> *Question:'What's important to teach?'*
> *Answer: 'It depends what you feel young people need to know and understand and be able to do to be successful in their lives.'*
>
> *Question: 'What do we mean by success?'*

So far we've looked at four of the five Key Questions — Why? What? Who? and How? The fifth – So What? – I want to delay for a while, and pick it up right at the end of this chapter as we head into Chapters Two and Three on Feedback and Feedforward.

A further reason for delay is the need right now to get closer to the dilemma which lies at the heart of educational assessment, and provide us with…

Big Idea Number 3:

Assessment choices face a dilemma – how to balance validity, reliability, manageability, and public acceptability.

Years ago I outlined this dilemma as I saw it at the time; experience of the past few years, in a number of education systems around the globe, has sharpened the issues even further. In 1991 I visualised it very simply:

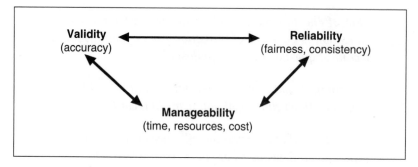

Now the same idea has taken on a slightly different shape, with the addition of a fourth factor – public acceptability – testifying to the increased political significance of assessment issues over the past decade.

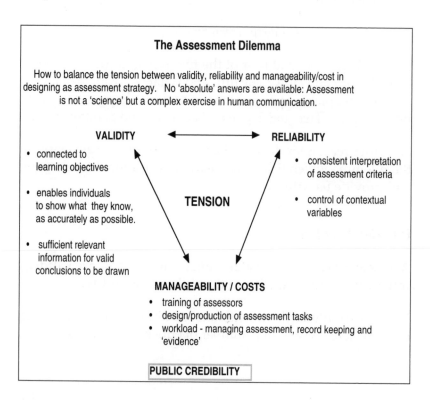

These four desirable features of any assessment process have to be held in balance. None of them are absolutes; none of them are perfectable; they are mutually incompatible and pull assessment design in different directions. No wonder we find the whole business so difficult, and if you crave quick solutions 'this way madness lies'.

Having ruled out easy solutions, however, closer examination of the dilemma may generate better understanding, and possibly some better choices.

What do we mean by 'Validity'?

In simple terms, validity is about the accuracy of the assessment. It implies two requirements. One is that the assessment tells you what you planned to find out about. The questions you ask, in whatever mode, should be central to what you have asked your students to learn, not about peripheral or irrelevant things, however easier those may be to assess. If you want your students to **understand** something, that's what you check for, not whether they just **know** it. The other requirement if the assessment is to be deemed valid/accurate is that the students (or whomever is being assessed) are enabled to show what they know, and not inhibited from doing so by the design or method of the assessment task or test.

Examples? Here's a couple from me – then you find some.

1. *You want to assess how well your students understand the character and motives of Hamlet, so you set them a task – 'You have 20 minutes, write all you can about the character of Hamlet.' When they've had twenty minutes, whether they have finished writing or not, you gather in the papers, read them and make a judgement about each student's understanding of Hamlet. One of the students, who wrote in detail about one aspect of Hamlet's character but nothing about anything else because he ran out of time, scores very low, even though you are clear that he has unusual insight*

> *and can support this with references to the text , if given a proper opportunity to do so. With a clearer task and more time, the assessment would have been a more valid reflection of the student's capability.*

The only, and frequently used, justification of such an assessment process is that it replicates the assessment method employed by the high-stake external examination later in the programme, but that too will generate an inaccurate picture of this student's ability, and in the meantime the student could have been so frustrated by the task that he learns the rules of the examination at the expense of his enthusiasm for the play.

2. *(a classic) The school (which was in the US) wanted to assess the students' creative writing, but only ever used multiple choice testing, and struggled to find a way to fit the two together. In the end they decided to identify the rules for successful creative writing, and then design a multiple choice test to check the student's knowledge of the rules. This was their solution to the assessment of creative writing.*

If you're interested in a much more detailed examination of the issue of validity in assessment, find an article in the journal 'Assessment in Education: Principles, Policy and Practice', vol. 3 number 3 (November 1996) by Terry Crooks, Michael Kane and Allan Cohen. The language is a bit technical in places but it's a really interesting view of assessment which calls much of our current practice into question. In particular, these three assessment experts recognise that the use of a range of assessment techniques may be the best way to ensure validity, as no one method alone can present a complete view of the student's actual learning.

One of the issues touched on in this article and in other recent thinking about assessment is the issue of 'sufficiency'. We know that valid assessment must comprehensively reflect the range of the learning being assessed, but how much evidence of learning is sufficient to say that a particular aspect of learning has been demonstrated? Strictly speaking, this is a validity issue, but it spills over into considerations of the reliability and credibility of the assessment process. Let me take an example from recent developments in New Zealand to illustrate this.

Some years ago New Zealand established an ambitious structure called the Qualifications Framework in an attempt to rationalise both academic and vocational qualifications and draw them together into one inclusive system of accreditation. The basis for the award of 'credit' is that the student (or the person in the workplace) has produced sufficient evidence of their achievement of the pre-stated standard. This evidence is judged by the teacher or workplace assessor.

Obviously, the process includes efforts to ensure the reliability of the assessment judgements being made, moderation procedures and so on.

Traditional academic assessment in New Zealand has been heavily reliant on external norm-referenced examinations, and has little experience of assessment decisions being made by teachers using evidence gathered in the classroom. The scepticism about the reliability of the new system has pushed the Qualifications Authority, who manage the scheme, into demanding lots of evidence of achievement, to establish a firm base for these high-stake judgements to be made. If they were more willing or able confidently to trust the judgement of the assessors, they might demand less evidence.

Consequently teachers involved in the new procedures find themselves gathering and checking large amounts of assessment evidence, and struggling with the manageability of this task, however committed they may be to the principles underpinning the Qualifications Framework. In this case, validity and reliability needs are both adding to the workload for the teachers, and the cost to the school. It's a problem

31

> *which needs to be resolved if New Zealand's young people*
> *are to be offered more valid ways of showing what they*
> *know and can do.*

The issue of 'sufficiency' therefore has become part of the dilemma in the 'standards-based' assessment systems currently being developed around the world. Over time it usually resolves itself, as the public as well as the educators and the students build their trust in new and previously unfamiliar assessment procedures. As their confidence in the process increases, the sheer quantity of evidence demanded gradually reduces, but it takes a while, and the first few years can be a rocky road, particularly for the teachers and students at the sharp end of the change.

What do we mean by 'Reliability'?

Basically, this is about consistency and fairness of our assessment. The question is, "If this assessment was used on a number of occasions to the same student, and marked/graded by different people each time, would the result be the same?"

Much of the effort and energy of the 'testing industry' in North America has been invested in this aim, with less attention paid to validity until very recently.

In order to achieve this aim, you have to control all the 'contextual variables' which might affect the outcome. All the rules regarding the adminstration of the test have to be carefully written and strictly followed. Great attention is paid to the wording to ensure that the students don't misunderstand the question. The design of multi-choice tests is taken extremely seriously. Why multi-choice? Because it can be scored by a computer using an optical mark reader thus removing the 'variable' of teacher error or interpretation.

I have an unfair caricature in my mind's eye of someone who regards reliability as the most important aspect of assessment design – sanitised, tidy, anxious about the messiness and unpredictability of the human condition. Their worst nightmare must be school-based assessment undertaken by teachers. There are so many variables, so much messiness and unpredictablity: teachers are so individualistic, and the children…it just doesn't bear thinking about.

Some of you may remember the first attempt to assess the hypothesising skills of seven year olds in English and Welsh schools. The development of such skills were an essential part of the Science curriculum, and should therefore have been assessed as carefully as anything else, to achieve a valid outcome. Instead of allowing teachers to judge the child's level of skill by informal observation over a period of time, the test developers wanted to create more controlled test conditions in the classroom, to improve the reliability of the exercise. Teachers were briefed carefully about the tasks they should give each child: in one case this involved asking the child to predict and explain whether and why certain items would sink or float in a tank of water strategically placed behind a screen in the corner of the classroom to avoid the other children witnessing each other's efforts. (I can already hear the collective groan of any of my readers who know about young children and tanks of water).

In classrooms all over the country, during the specified week, the story was the same, water everywhere, teachers trying to manage the questioning of each child while keeping an eye on the rest of the class. Countless stories emerged of the funny and not so funny happenings which transpired..

One of the items to be 'tested' in the water tank was a banana. By the end of the week some of the bananas had had enough. 'Now then Jonathan,' said the teacher to the 29th child, 'here's a banana, do you think it will sink or float?' Jonathan was a bright boy. He'd watched and listened all week as the rest of the class had their date with destiny and

33

the water tank. The word on the street was that the banana floated, the only dispute was about why it did so. His turn had come. The now water-logged banana was placed in the tank – and sank like a stone to the bottom, weighted down by saturation. Jonathan watched in disbelief. 'Damn', he said.

One of the horns of the dilemma we face in educational assessment is this tension between the need to assess the important things not just the assessable things, and the potential unreliability of some of the assessment methods which result from this pursuit of validity. After the fun and games of floating and sinking in the classroom, the test developers gave up the idea of controlling all the assessment circumstances and left the assessment of these skills to the observation and judgement of the teachers, while more structured ways were found of checking the content knowledge of the children.

A compromise has evolved in National Curriculum assessment in England and Wales, involving external standardised testing of some of the curriculum together with the requirement on teachers to assess the students' achievement using a wide range of techniques over a number of events and drawing conclusions about the 'level' which best reflects the consistent achievement. These results are published side by side with the test results, reflecting as they do two quite different views. Done well, Teacher Assessment (that is the assessments conducted by the teachers in their own classrooms) can reflect a more accurate and valid view than the test result alone. Done badly, it can be unreliable and therefore unfair to the student.

In order to improve the reliability of Teacher Assessment, therefore, the national assessment agency now requires schools to undertake 'standardising' activities, to bring into line with each other the teachers' interpretations of the wording of the 'standard' and the evidence they would expect of its achievement. To do this, examples of students work are used as the basis of in-school discussion, and exemplars of agreed standards are kept to inform teachers' judgement. These 'standards portfolios' can then be shared among schools, to ease the standards in different schools and districts into line with each other.

This is a pretty herculean effort: if its only impact was to improve the fairness of teachers' assessment that would be a worthy aim, but expensive. In fact, in my experience, the actual outcome of this process has been to make teachers talk to each other about the learning tasks they provide for their students, about how students learn and demonstrate their learning, about the judgements we make about learning all day every day, and the action we take as a result. There are few things more important for teachers to discuss.

A system designed to improve reliability has actually made a real contribution to validity too, because the question for teachers is often about the design of assessment tasks. How do we create tasks which will encourage and enable our students not only to learn but to show what they know? That's a great question.

Manageability and Cost

No assessment can be absolutely valid, unless we find a way to scan the brains of our students to discover exactly what they know and understand in relation to the things we are trying to find out about. No assessment can be absolutely reliable, however hard we try to remove the human factor altogether. Assessment, after all, is an exercise in human communication: all we can do is endeavour to make it as accurate and fair as possible, and then admit to the limitations of the process, not hide its inadequacies behind an elaborate mask of certainty.

Manageability is a crucial part of the assessment equation for the teachers and students who have to make the assessment process work in the messy reality of schools. In their case the main cost is time, to prepare, administer and sometimes to grade or score the results. As we have already seen, improving the validity of classroom assessment may mean talking to students rather than have them write all the time. Improving the reliability of assessment takes time too, especially when the standards to be used are expressed in words which assessors must interpret consistently. Unless teachers and schools think through their assessment strategies very carefully, they may be tempted by the most manageable options and reduce the quality of their assessment as a result. Careful planning, and awareness of the issues involved can help to resolve the problem, but it remains a compromise which may be uncomfortable for people who like everything clear and simple. The suggestion from Terry Crooks, a New Zealand expert on assessment design whose work has already been mentioned, is to consider what would be the most valid way to form a judgement about learning, and then work backwards from that ideal until you reach a manageable strategy, rather than starting with manageability and trying to make it more valid.

On the larger level of the state or the province the cost is financial: tests have to be commissioned and designed, papers printed and distributed, assessors trained, parents informed – these costs are very considerable, and expand as the assessment process becomes more complicated.

Now the dilemma becomes both sharp and central to the political arena. Teachers may object collectively to the extra work required to assess students themselves and to administer external assessment. The Treasury may object to the use of public money to pursue a more complex (and probably more valid) assessment process when traditional methods would have been cheaper. These interests may combine: when in 1993 in England and Wales teacher unions objected to the workload implications of school-based assessment of the National Curriculum, the government agreed to pay for the scoring of the tests, using

money which had been set aside for improving the quality of teachers' own assessments. This may have been a win-win solution for the teachers and the government, but the loser may have been the most valid opportunity for many students to show what they know.

Public Acceptability

From time to time during this chapter I have referred to 'traditional' approaches to assessment, which are now being challenged by new ways of expressing the curriculum, a new focus on specific information about learning, and growing recognition of the limitations of external testing as the only means of checking learning. I have mentioned in the Preface the ambivalence felt by many politicians' dealing with education policy: do they want to look forward to teaching and assessment methods relevant to to the next century, or back to the methods of the past century? Parents and grandparents, who are also voters and therefore never far from the politicians concerns, are also caught in this dilemma. They want or need to know where their child or grandchild stands in some norm-based order of merit, but they can only really help with the improvement of learning if they understand more explicitly what has been learned, and what is still to be done.

The wider public, including those with a personal stake in the education system, have all experienced school and assessment as part of their childhood, and have views about what works and what doesn't. The issues are never neutral, and childhood experiences often leave a legacy of emotion attached to questions of testing and examinations. The 11+ selection examination may be a thing of the past in most of the UK, but it has left its mark on my generation in terms of our educational opportunities, and even our academic self-esteem.

Major changes in national, state or provincial assessment do, therefore, concern many adults as well as students. Assessment methods, particularly for high-stake purposes, affect families and make headlines. If parents object strongly enough, policy makers have to listen. In 1993, when assessment in England and Wales caused such anger among teachers, it was the objections of school governing bodies and many individual parents which led to the review of the offending arrangements, and subsequent revisions. In California too, the secrecy and complexity of the California Learning Assessment System (CLAS) in 1993 and 1994, compounded by general anti-government feeling, caused sufficient parental objections for the State Governor finally to veto the proposals.

Distrust in teachers too, which has been a feature of some government rhetoric over the past decade, has led to a feeling that school-based assessments, conducted by teachers, do not produce credible results. This was the argument put forward for disallowing 100% coursework for some British GCSE examinations. The evidence that these methods had clearly increased the motivation and performance of some students was overridden by citing 'public unease' and a demand for 'more rigorous' external examinations. A similar argument has been a feature of the New Zealand Qualifications Framework, as I mentioned earlier.

Even at the level of an individual school, decisions about assessment strategies must take account of the reactions of students and their parents to what may be unfamiliar ideas, however worthy their teachers consider the new plans to be. Parents worry understandably about their children being used as guinea-pigs for new-fangled notions of unproven worth. Their touchstones for quality may be their own experiences ten or twenty years ago, but that's understandable too if no-one has helped them to understand why and how educational change has happened, and its implications for their children.

National or state level policy-makers have a duty to explain, but may not do so as clearly or explicitly as many parents want or need. The rest of the explanation rests with schools, one more thing for busy people to do, but eminently worth-while. Anything which establishes or reinforces the partnership between student, family and school in raising achievement is worth doing, because the investment of time pays off.

Finding the 'Best Fit' between validity, reliability, manageability and public acceptability

Time and again, in explaining the components of these 'best fit' decisions we have come across examples of the dilemmas faced by assessment designers, in the classroom as well as in national or provincial assessment systems. We have seen how the most valid assessment is often the hardest to manage. Improvements in the reliability of assessment have also often meant more and different work for teachers and schools, and headaches for those planning to reduce contextual variables in the unpredictable circumstances of the school. We have also begun to understand how the personal education experience of all of us can affect our perceptions of the assessment process, making us trust or distrust the status quo, or the developing changes. Assessment issues are never value-free: they involve difficult choices, with serious consequences for those being assessed. The dilemma is real, and deserves every bit of the intelligence and time it takes to find the necessary compromises. Absolute solutions are unattainable: that fact alone is a worry to those who like to see things 'fixed' and under control.

If you've been keeping different assessment issues – such as teacher appraisal or school evaluation – in your mind while reading this chapter, my hope is that some insights will be emerging already about implications and ways forward. In later chapters we will deal explicitly with the application of these ideas to those issues. In the meantime, we have one more key question to consider, picking up from page 27.

Question Five: So What? ... What do we do with the information when we have it?

With thought and care we have gathered some assessment information which is as accurate and fair as we can manage in the circumstances which surround us. But 'weighing the pig doesn't make it grow': assessment does not necessarily lead to improvement in either teaching or learning. We have first to communicate about learning to the students, to each other or to ourselves, and then we have to use the information to decide what to do next. **Feedback and feedforward: two essential concomitants of sound assessment which deserve two chapters all to themselves.**

Key Points

1. **Assessment should actually improve learning not just measure it.**

2. **The five assessment assessment questions are Why? What? Who? How? and So What?**

3. **A balance has to be found between the often conflicting demands of validity, reliability, manageability, cost and public acceptability.**

One big question:

What four phrases would you use to describe 'teaching', and in what order of priority?

Chapter Two:
Feedback

In Chapter One we looked at the need to gather good information about learning, and defined 'good' as 'clearly relevant to what you wanted to find out about, accurate, fair, and sufficient to enable conclusions to be drawn'. In order for the outcome of the assessment to be valued there is also a need to understand and respect the process : without such respect the information which results may be under-valued, and therefore have less impact.

This chapter is concerned with how this assessment information is communicated to all those interested in learning and improvement. This may be feedback to the learner him/herself, oral or written, or both ; to the teacher ; to the parent and family and anyone else interested in the learner's improvement. We shall look at different types of feedback, the use of words and codes, the methods and timing involved, the usefulness and use made of the feedback. Some of the advice and suggestions will come from the common sense and experience of the teachers and schools I've worked with over the years. There's a fair amount of academic research to call upon too, and I'll refer to it when it's interesting and helpful.

Here again, as in Chapter One, the examples offered will be mostly to do with our assessment of students, but as you read keep your mind open to the implications for feedback to teachers as adult learners : later chapters will pick up such issues explicitly, but you don't have to wait till then to start thinking about them. The whole point of 'The Learning School' is that everyone - adult and child - in the school is learning, all the time.

I'm going to offer first a rather bald list of the characteristics of effective feedback, drawn from a variety of sources, and then explore them in greater depth. The order of these is not significant, but I've numbered them for ease of reference. If you wish, make your own list, based on your own experience and common sense and see how they compare. Think about yourself as a learner receiving feedback as well as a teacher offering it.

Effective feedback should:

1. be descriptive rather than evaluative;

2. be specific, and both positive and critical;

3. be offered as soon as possible after the event to which it refers;

4. encourage and plan for opportunities for the feedback to be used, as soon as possible in the first instance;

5. look forward to the next specific steps to improve 'performance';

6. offer alternatives, or ask the learner to do so;

7. involve the learner wherever possible, to improve the chance of the feedback being understood and acted upon;

8. address the learning, not the person.

Descriptive and Evaluative, Positive and Critical

In their 1994 study of the feedback offered to young children in primary school classrooms, Caroline Gipps and Pat Tunstall outline the various types which emerged from their observations:

> "*verbal and non-verbal; distinctly positive or negative feedback; process and product related feedback; feedback which was based on the use or non-use of explicit criteria; feedback which related to extrinsic or intrinsic motivation;*

> *feedback related to encouragement; feedback in different curriculum areas; feedback which related to distinctly personal style; feedback to individual children; feedback which involved different relationships; feedback as part of classroom management."*

Like many other researchers in this field, Gipps and Tunstall also distinguish usefully between **evaluative** and **descriptive** feedback. Evaluative feedback offers a judgement about the learning, sometimes expressed in words, sometimes expressed in a code - grade, mark or score - although the latter is much more common in secondary schools. The words will be evaluative words such as 'excellent' or 'poor' or 'satisfactory'. The judgement may be comparing the student's work to the work of other students, or the comparison may be with the expected standard or norms, which may or may not be made explicit to the learner. Evaluative feedback often includes judgements about the attitude and effort of the learner.

Descriptive feedback offers information about the specific task, how it was undertaken and the characteristics of the result. It tends to be more neutral in tone, and is much more explicit about expectations or standards. Codes are used less because they are less explicit and specific than is usual with descriptive feedback. There is more emphasis too on the cognitive aspects of what the learner has done, and less comment on effort and attitude.

In terms of the day to day activities of teachers, talking to children, marking or grading their work and discussing it with them, these distinctions are really useful. They're useful too in considering how we write about students' learning for others - their parents, or the next teacher or school, or even an employer or university admissions person. The choice of which style to use seems to revolve around our purpose in providing feedback or in writing about achievement. If the purpose is summative - to summarise, or judge, or categorise, or compare, then evaluative information may be appropriate. But if our purpose is to improve learning, or to help someone else understand the learner's needs, then we should use evaluative feedback only if we believe that such feedback actually improves learning. Otherwise, we would need to provide the specific, explicit feedback which has a chance of helping the learner to know how to improve their work.

One way to check your own views here is to consider yourself as a learner - in any situation not just academic learning - and the kind of feedback you need to improve your learning. You'll probably recall the feedback you've been given over the years and recognise some of it as really helpful and some of it as not helpful at all. In fact, some feedback - both 'positive' and 'negative' - can be so unhelpful that it actually undermines your incentive to carry on learning.

This may be a good opportunity to tackle the long-running argument about 'positive' and 'negative' feedback to learners and teachers writing about them. The issue may be cultural - the British seem to be more suspicious of positive feedback than the Americans, for example - but we might have to ask whether habit has created culture or the other way round. Some societies are more 'critical' than others, more sparing with praise and more wary of being publically congratulated. The New Zealanders have what they call the 'tall poppy' syndrome, which refers to their tendency to want to cut down to size anyone whose achievements elevate them above their peers. But beyond all these rather fatalistic and stereotypical expectations, there are other patterns at work.

Some traditional patterns of teaching did not regard assessment and feedback as part of learning and therefore not an essential part of the teacher's job. The teacher was in personal control of the teaching process and the learners had to work out for themselves the specifics of what was required, through trial and error and very close attention to the implicit expectations of the teacher. Reward and punishment were used to add extrinsic motivation to the search for the right answer. Children who were particularly attentive or insightful worked out the requirements for themselves and were rewarded ; others did not and were not. Large classes also militated against specific feedback because of the time it takes, and the focus on the specific learning of specific students doing specific tasks.

Some of the same logistical pressures remain, but a number of recent developments have made teachers reconsider the feedback they offer. One of these developments was **Records of Achievement.** In the 1980s in the UK, encouraged by the Department of Employment and the Technical and Vocational Education Initiative (TVEI) many teachers began to offer more specific feedback to their students, and helped students to become more involved in their learning, assessment and target-setting. Periodic review of learning was implemented, leading to the Record of Achievement which school-leavers would take with them into the work-place or into further education and training. The National Record of Achievement, containing statements about and evidence of achievement, became part of the school experience for many students.

The summative Record of Achievement was like a passport into the next stage of the student's life: as such the statements developed by both school and individual students were to be a positive reflection of achievement to date, together with an individual action plan for the student's future. Some schools and teachers interpreted this emphasis on the positive to mean that the formative years leading up to the summative Record of Achievement should also generate only positive statements of the student's performance, with critical analysis regarded as 'negative' and therefore inappropriate. Clearly a distinction needs to be seen between the final Record of Achievement, the purpose of which is exacly that - to record achievement - and the formative learning process underpinning this summative statement.

In a sense the argument has been about the wrong issue. The real issue in feedback and in writing about learning is not 'positive or negative' but 'evaluative or descriptive. Descriptive feedback is about the specifics of performance, not just about whether the performance is 'good' or 'bad. This is what a local employer said to me while we were explaining the Record of Achievement to our colleagues in the community. 'You teachers, ' he said, ' seem obsessed with judging students. People are different: I want to know about these young people to decide whether or not they have the skills I need. Just tell me about them, their work habits, whether they like to work alone or with others, whether they're quiet or sociable, but leave me to do the judgement.' He wanted description, not evaluation.

A further relevant development has been the introduction and nature of the **The National Curriculum.** As we've mentioned before, many states and provinces around the world now have a more specific and explicit required curriculum than was previously in place. This curriculum is in the public domain : it can be bought over the counter by parents or students or anyone else who's interested in what young people are being taught in school. Because the curriculum itself is specific and explicit, teachers can be so with their students, as they outline tasks and their relevance to the curriculum requirements and as they give feedback and suggest how work can be improved. In these days of published results it is clearly in the interests of schools and teachers for students' learning and performance to be improved. If being more specific helps towards that end, then let's do it.

These developments have created a curious irony which is worth exploring briefly. It is clearly empowering to students to give them more information about what is expected of them, and specific feedback which will guide them towards improvement. But only up to a point. Student's own learning pathways and preferences may not mesh exactly with the pathways and expectations laid down in the required curriculum and explained by their teachers. By providing too much specific guidance and feedback we may actually be stultifying the student's personal learning agenda, and creating a whole generation of over-convergent learners. As ever, balance and variety are needed, and a recognition that no one way of doing anything in education will always be right for all your students. No quick-fix solutions, no absolute rules: the best teachers think and listen, reflect, set high expectations, challenge orthodoxies.

Before moving on, let me offer one more way of considering the evaluative/descriptive, positive/negative issues in feedback. Consider the notion of teaching as an exercise in power and control. If this control is exercised through rewards and punishment, then it is in the teacher's interest to keep the criteria for assessment to herself. As these criteria can be surmised through specific feedback, feedback must remain non-specific too. Only then will the learners have no way of challenging the teacher's judgement. You may reject such notions utterly as an insult to your motives and methods in teaching, but think about the way you perceived some of the teachers you have encountered in your learning life. This is not to advocate disorder in the classroom or to suggest that teachers and students are on an absolutely equal footing, which is clearly not the case. I suggest merely that our decisions about the type of feedback we offer to learners may stem from some quite complex motives, and these need to be explored if we are to decide which methods are the most likely to improve learning, which is after all the core purpose of the school.

The Use of Codes, Grades, Marks, and other 'Short-hand' in Feedback

Clearly, codes as feedback are mainly associated with evaluative methods rather than descriptive. We need to consider, however, whether these codes are attached to explicit criteria, and could therefore be 'de-coded' to reveal more descriptive information. Take a typical code of - a grade 'B', or 7/10. On its own, related to nothing, it offers nothing to the student except the vaguest idea that their work is better than a C and not as good as an A. They know that they should aim for an A but don't really know what an A entails or how to achieve it. 'Try harder' says the teacher, but try harder at what? Many teachers assume that students really do know what to do to improve their work and choose not to do it, but such assumptions need checking.

If on the other hand the codes are a short-hand expression of more explicit expectations which have been shared effectively with the students, then the use of such codes as a form of communicating between teacher and learners may be more fruitful.

> *On the classroom wall is a chart showing the key characteristics of work which could earn a certain grade or mark or score. Examples have been offered to illuminate these statements of expectations, and they have been discussed and explained further when necessary. If then the teacher communicates with her students about past or future learning in terms of codes attached to these explicit and specific statements, we have gone beyond evaluation into description.*

Timing: feedback should be offered as soon as possible after the event to which it is related, and early opportunities are needed for the feedback to be used.

Informal feedback, verbal and non-verbal, is being offered constantly in classrooms and other learning environments. By word, gesture, in all sorts of ways, teachers let their students know what they think about their learning and their effort and response and behaviour. The teachers in Gipps and Tunstall's project used all sorts of methods as they worked with their six and seven-year old children. "Children, I've got to use my big voice again, " said one teacher, her meaning quite unmistakeable. Feedback was immediate - no issues of timing there.

As soon as children reach the stage where their learning can be demonstrated on paper and therefore assessed by the teacher at a distance from them, feedback tends to become more formal, written, and detached from the actual learning. This distance and relative detachment may allow space for reflection and more considered feedback rather than the immediate response, but there are potential problems here too which we need to examine. 'Marking' and 'grading' constitute a large proportion of many teachers' workloads: time spent on them cannot be spent on other things. If teachers are to spend precious energy on ensuring that students get useful feedback, we have to be confident that the feedback will make a difference.

To gather information about evidence concerning the impact of feedback on students I've used a review of the world research evidence in this area, compiled in 1988 by Terry Crooks, the New Zealand assessment expert I've mentioned before. As you might expect, the review is pretty lengthy, but it's rich in information and constantly mentioned in more recent works on assessment. Terry identifies three key characteristics of effective feedback: in the conclusion to the article he writes:

> *"First, feedback is most effective if it focuses students' attention on their progress in mastering educational tasks. Such emphasis on personal progress enhances self-efficacy, encourages effort attributions, and reduces attention to social comparison. The approach that leads to the most valuable feedback is nicely captured by Easley and Zwoyer (1975):*
>
> > *'If you can both listen to children and accept their answers not as things to be judged right or wrong but as pieces of information which may reveal what the child is thinking you will have taken a giant step toward becoming a master teacher rather than merely a disseminator of information.'*
>
> *Second, feedback should take place while it is still clearly relevant. This usually implies that it should be provided*

soon after a task is completed, and that the student should be given opportunities subsequently to demonstrate learning from the feedback. One of the strengths of mastery learning approaches is the emphasis on feedback and subsequent opportunities to correct deficiencies without penalty for the earlier failure.

Third, feedback should be specific and related to need. Simple knowledge of results should be provided consistently (directly or implicitly), with more detailed feedback only where necessary to help the student work through misconceptions or other weaknesses in performance. Praise should be used sparingly and where used should be task specific, whereas criticism (other than simply identifying deficiencies) is usually counterproductive"

Sorry about the 'master teacher' bit by the way, but it was 1975: incidentally, the research study which prompted the advice was done in Maths classes.

The first and last of Terry's points here tally with the outcomes from Gipps and Tunstall referred to earlier. I want to take the second point and explore its implications. Feedback should be offered as soon as possible after the event.

Every instinct tells us the same. Immediate feedback is highly effective, but rarely manageable in the reality of the amount of work produced, the numbers of students, and the time at our disposal. If ever you can and do manage it, marking the student's work soon after its completion, with the student alongside you, discussing the work as you go along, is undoubtedly more effective than taking it away and returning it sometime later.

More likely is the scenario where the work is completed and handed in, taken away for 'marking' or 'grading' (same task, different continent) and returned. If the students are working in books which they use for their normal classwork you may try to turn the marking round before the students use these books again, but more likely work will accumulate for a week or two, or even longer, before you find the time to check it all, write whatever feedback you have time for in a little note to the student, and return it. When the work is returned you may spend time going through it with them, individually or as a group, but the pressures of the required curriculum may oblige you to move on, leaving the students just time to compare their grades before they too move on, switching their focus to the new work. It seems like a relentless treadmill, and you may have a nagging suspicion that the carefully chosen words you wrote on the students' work as you marked it may not even be read, never mind acted upon. And you'd probably be right.

Depressing isn't it. We can shrug your shoulders about it and carry on regardless, or we can apply our collective intelligence to finding a way of providing faster feedback without resorting to the briefest amount to achieve a quicker turn-round.

Lateral thinking required. Possible solutions:

1. Set less written work, and you'll have less to mark. Sounds heretical, but students in UK secondary schools at least do a phenomenal amount of writing during their school careers, and could without doubt do less without damage to their academic development, if we could persuade them and their parents that 'working' doesn't necessarily involve 'writing'. Have you ever had the experience of doing something really useful and stimulating in the classroom which involved discussion, or visual work, or role play, and then the students ask if they're going to do any work today?

2. Establish two 'levels' of marking: one is fast, impressionistic or focussed on one characteristic only, and is used to check basic criteria such as completion. It clearly indicates to the students that their work has been looked at and that their effort in producing it has been recognised. This relatively

superficial feedback is enhanced by much more detailed checking periodically with specific, explicit feedback provided for each student. You might choose to focus in detail on the work of a subset of the whole group on a kind of rolling programme, so each student gets a share of your very specific attention and advice. The challenge is to decide how frequently the detailed feedback should be offered, and the maximum turn-round time involved, and stick to it. Call this **the students' entitlement to detailed feedback to improve their learning** and it becomes an issue for all teachers, not just individuals or particular teams.

3. Train the students from the earliest possible age to 'mark' (but not necessarily grade) their own and each others' work. The purpose is definitely descriptive rather than evaluative, and students need help to learn how to do this effectively : it's a learned skill. From the age of eight or nine onwards, and even earlier given the right prompts and structures, children are offered specific guidance about the desired qualities and characteristics in their work, both the process and the product. If necessary we show them what it would look like if it was good, or brilliant, or just OK and let them think and talk about what they need to do to achieve these standards. Address quite explicitly and with their help the kind of feedback they want and need and deserve if their learning is to improve. They could draw up, with or without your help, their own guidelines for effective feedback - which will probably be very close to the accumulated wisdom of the researchers. If they get stuck or need your help, advise them : if they're going seriously off-track, and the impact of their proposals might be damaging to some in your opinion, set the boundaries. You have a right to your say just as they have a right to theirs. When you have some agreed guidelines for effective feedback, write them up big and put them on the wall.

Give the students some 'scaffolding' for their early attempts at high-quality feedback. When their learning in this area is more assured you can gradually remove the scaffolding and the structure will remain, unsupported. If we aim to make our students autonomous learners by the age of 18 if not 16, then the process starts early, and includes making them autonomous assessors of their own work, and able to encourage and support the learning of others. What a useful skill that is, in all sorts of contexts.

In the early stages, after you've discussed what's useful feedback, and discussed it in relation to a given task, hand out to all of them some examples of the completed task produced by a previous year, or in another school, and assess it together, correcting it, offering alternatives and next steps to improvement. You model the process with their help; next time they model the process with your help; next time they work on it together in a group and swap over to check their conclusions, and so it goes, until practice and good feedback improves the skill.

Then, and only when the skills have been developed in this way, the students will be ready to share the feedback task with you. You've invested time in teaching them these skills, now comes the pay-off. Of course you will want to cross-check the feedback they give to each other or to themselves, to ensure that they're on track and improving their standards. And there will be areas of their work when you will want to provide the feedback yourself, now that some of it is provided by them under your supervision. You will want to review with individual students or small groups. You may need to remind all the students about the guidelines periodically, or suggest that they be reviewed and sharpened in the light of experience.

All these possibilities were stimulated by considering how to reduce the time delay between work being done and feedback being received. Now you have a system which could support more timely feedback, by sharing the task with the students rather than doing it all yourself. It will take time out of the classroom, which may mean adjusting your plans to create class time for it. You may end up teaching a little less, but the students may still learn a little more. It's not a case of 'effective feedback **or** improved exam/test results' but rather 'effective feedback **as a means to** improved exam/test results'.

4. Once these skills are established they can be used to tackle the issue of the timing of feedback. Feedback can now be generated by the students themselves, soon after a task has been completed, using time that you have planned for. This feedback - clear, specific, descriptive - will be completed with specific suggestions for improvement.   Once the feedback and suggestions have been shared, considered and discussed you could carry straight through to a re-draft of the work in question, or a part of it, to incorporate the feedback and improve on the first attempt. The first round of feedback was aimed entirely at improvement. When the students ask "Do we get a mark for this?" the answer is, "No, but you do get the chance to improve on the mark you would have got." The second attempt can be scored or graded if your assessment strategy requires it, and can be marked by you if it's a high-stake piece and the students and their parents need the extra comfort of your expertise.

5. In order to achieve the benefits of reducing the time between task, feedback and re-draft you need to regard this process as part of the planned learning in the topic, module or chunk of learning, not an extra chore at the end. The nature of our teaching programme may mean that the key learning in one chunk may not be referred to in the next : this is particularly true when teaching is focussed on particular content rather than more generic concepts and skills.

Feedback in these cases needs to be encompassed within the time frame of the chunk, not spilling over into the next one where it may seem marginal and unrelated to the current focus. More than ever, we plan assessment as an integral part of the teaching and learning programme.

Keeping Track of Feedback, and 'Next Steps'

If we are aiming for more specific feedback, we're into words as well as or as a substitute for codes - grades, scores and so on. Right from the outset, that fact alone challenges the ways in which we have traditionally kept track, in our mark or grade books. I say 'traditionally', but record-keeping habits seem to die hard and I'm constantly surprised that the formats of many teachers' record books don't seem to have changed much over the years, despite quite radical changes in the curriculum which underpins them.

Basically, the pages of small boxes have got to go. You need more space to keep track of more specific things, which may mean fewer bigger boxes, or using disc rather than paper, or records per student rather than per class. I've written elsewhere about different kinds of record-keeping (Assessment for Learning, 1995, pages 71–82): suffice to add here one strategy I found in a school, which you might want to try.

At the back of each student's work book or folder was a record sheet:

Date	Task	Feedback 'mark' plus comments	Next step(s) 'SMART' targets	Parent comments

As each piece of work was assessed and returned, the students, under the teacher's supervision, would complete the record with the date of the piece, a concise decription of the task, the feedback they had received including both mark, grade, and specific feedback either written or oral. If necessary the students would re-read the comments on their work from their teacher and copy them out again. At least they'd been required to notice them, and not be blinded by the grade alone. Then by discussion with you, or a 'learning partner' or just on reflection, the student writes in a specific next step which will improve their work next time. The record sheet will go to and from school with the work book or folder in the normal course of events. The parent or other adult interested in the student's progress then has the chance to comment, on the task, the feedback, the target, or all three. If the teacher wishes to see all the feedback and targets she gathers in all the workbooks and can find the summary quickly and without difficulty, as can anyone else in school interested in the work and progress of an individual student, the whole group or a sample of the students. It's a one-write multi-purpose method of keeping track, produced by each student for him/herself. It's cheap, simple and potentially very effective.

It also brings me round to another of the characteristics for effective feedback which were listed at the beginning of this chapter.

Involving the learner wherever possible in the feedback, to improve the chance of it being understood and acted upon.

We've already established that training and encouraging students to be involved can help with some of the logistical problems of feedback, but manageability alone is not enough. We have to believe that involving learners will actually improve their learning, the core purpose which lies at the heart of all that schools and teachers do.

Many of us, thinking about our own learning experiences, will feel that real learning only happens when it's understood, remembered for more than a few days, built on and consolidated. How do we achieve this? Teachers have been concerned about this for as long as teaching has existed. We are conscientious and work hard to try and achieve this aim. Sometimes we can actually try too hard.

Let me return for a while to the two key studies of the impact of assessment and feedback on students and learning, to see if we can underpin this intuition with any firm evidence. In his comprehensive review of the evidence, Terry Crooks emphasises the need for deep learning, the avoidance of 'grading on a curve' until the final year or two of high school, the need for clear specific feedback, the benefits of student cooperation, the need to offer students choice of learning and assessment activities, and so on. He does not talk explicitly about self assessment as the answer, nor about the mechanics of involving students in this process. But the images of teaching and learning which emerge from this study are still clearly focussed on treating students as individuals, encouraging intrinsic motivation and improved 'self-efficacy', involving a partnership between teacher and learners, while leaving no doubt that the expertise about teaching still rests with the teacher.

Perhaps what we are doing here is re-defining or clarifying what we mean by 'teaching'. It is more than instruction and induction into a body of knowledge. The students are not empty vessels waiting to be filled up: they already have ideas and experiences on which teaching must build, and the teacher's job is to connect to what's already there, identify it, shape it, push it along. It's a two way communication, with both sides listening carefully to each other. If one of the parties becomes too dominant, it might make the other too passive.

This was the issue picked up by Gipps and Tunstall in their study of feedback in the primary school. We have seen how they identified that specific feedback related to particular learning seemed to have a greater impact than more generalised evaluative feedback. Another area they explored was the relative role of teacher and child in deciding what had been learned well and what was still to be done. In their 'typology' of feedback, Types A and B were both basically evaluative, Types C and D more clearly descriptive. Type C was very much driven by the teacher, who acknowledged attainment, offered criteria, corrected errors and modelled appropriate responses. This type of feedback did have a positive impact on the next learning of the children who received it. But it was Type D feedback which appeared to maximise improvement, and Type D demanded more of the children. The strategies employed in this category ranged from discussing work with the child, to suggesting rather than dictating next steps, through to expecting the child to self-correct.

If you know about the Reading Recovery programme which has a considerable effect on the improvement of reading in primary schools in New Zealand and other parts of the world, you will already know about one of the guiding principles whereby the young readers are asked to correct their own mistakes, to work out for themselves what went wrong and how to put it right. If your instinct as a teacher is always to correct error as a way of helping the student you may need to take a deep breath over this. What Gipps and Tunstall found were teachers who expected children to correct their own mistakes, if they believed they knew how to do so, and waited until they did, rather than intervene too soon to put it right. For this to happen the teacher had to trust in the capability of the child, and also have the patience to see that trust rewarded.

> *Watching Reading Recovery in operation in a Wellington primary school some years ago I sat in on the first session between a Reading Recovery tutor and her 'client', a boy who had just been screened at his sixth birthday and selected for the programme. He was a relaxed affable boy, youngest of a large family, comfortable with adults. The session began and he was asked to read, which he began to do. Once or twice he stumbled and corrected himself. Then*

he got really stuck. 'That's not right, is it ' said the teacher and he agreed that it was not. 'Try and put it right,' she said. He tried, but nothing happened. 'Keep trying', she said. A long silence ensued. He gazed at the page for a while and then turned and gazed at the teacher, expecting that she would now help him out. She stared out of the window. Then he turned and smiled at me, certain that someone would help him. We were both teachers after all and that's what teachers do. I felt my pulse rate go up. I wanted to help him, but knew I shouldn't. By now his smile had turned to puzzlement. The silence continued. Minutes had passed. Finally it dawned on the boy that neither of us was going to help him, and he turned back to the book. Slowly, painfully, he began to work it out, using everything he'd ever been told about how letters fit together, which he probably thought he'd forgotten. At last he tried again and got it right. All of us smiled, his tutor congratulated him warmly as he did it again, just to make sure. He'd done it, and his faith in his own ability to read pushed him on to tackle the next hurdle, and the next. He's probably forgotten all about that incident now, but I haven't.

Very few of us in education would claim that self-correction is always possible or appropriate, but we might also ask ourselves how often our students are offered a real opportunity to work it out for themselves, and then allowed to do so without premature interruption from a teacher who is either very anxious to help or simply too busy to wait. It's hard to listen patiently, asking prompting but not leading questions, while the classroom carries on around you and you want to 'get on'. Good classroom management matters of course, and so, I believe, does class size.

One final thing, before we move on to consider feedback to other potential audiences, beyond the students and their teacher. Parents and caregivers who play a key role in supporting learning, are another major audience for good information about the student's progress, strengths and difficulties. Their information will be provided periodically by the school, but not as frequently as feedback is available in the classroom, and probably not in as much detail either. Schools in all systems have to meet clear statutory responsibilities and minimum standards of reporting, but these do vary, and the development of more specific standards or outcomes—based curriculums makes quite a difference too.

More specific and explicit teaching requirements lead quite naturally to more specific and explicit ways of recording and communicating learning. This in turn may well increase the sheer volume of information to be gathered and shared, and some schools have understandably sought to stream-line this process by making one information system fit all the various audiences. If, for example, information about learning is needed by students, the current teacher, the next teacher or school, and the parents, it sounds tempting to pursue a once-for-all method of recording, which can be turned into different formats for different audiences.

I'm always interested in systems that will genuinely save time and energy, but I'm not convinced that this urge for integrating information systems really works. Here's a true story to illustrate the problem.

> *The school in question was a large secondary school where the teachers had worked hard to improve their classroom assessment and feedback, as part of their aim to improve learning and teaching. Each team had worked on appropriate ways to help students understand the specific strengths and weaknesses of their work, and feedback was offered continually as part of the normal activity and conversation in the classroom. There were no fixed structures or timings: it was suited to the circumstances which prevailed at the time, and it was beginning to work well, in that students were beginning to take more responsibility for the improvement of their work, assisted by their teachers.*

Enter a Deputy Head with an interest in systems and a brief to monitor the school's reporting system. Obviously the classroom process was generating useful information about learning and next steps, just what the school wanted to offer to parents, so why not meet both purposes and audiences at once. There would have to be slight adjustments though for information which was going to go beyond the school. It would have to be 'tidied up' for a start, and there would need to be an agreed 'format' used by everybody. And of course it would be really messy to have information for different subjects going home at different times - but apart from that, everything would be just the same.

*What the school quickly discovered was when you add parents to the list of receivers of information, their needs begin to undermine the original purpose of the exercise. More emphasis began to be placed on the cosmetics, uniformity and simultaneity of information — sharing than on the need to make the information support daily laerning in the classroom. Instead of providing feedback as and when it was useful, specified dates were allocated for sending information home - in addition of course to the twice yearly report. A working group representing different subject teams was set up to agree a common format, but the Art department was not at all happy that this would mean the end of its well-designed system which suited their needs perfectly. They were not convinced that they could do their own thing **in addition to** the system now required by the school.*

After almost a year of disagreements, the school had reached no more than an uncomfortable compromise about the format and timing of the new system while the original subject-specific ways of working had begun to fade, giving way to the higher stake process.

They would have done better to leave well alone, fully integrate good assessment and feedback into the daily habits of teaching, and to have thought about improving the information for parents as a separate issue.

Parents need specific information and suggestions about useful next steps involving teachers, students and home, but they need a summary periodically, rather than all the daily details which make most sense to the two parties immersed in the every day learning - teachers and students.

The frameworks of the new state and provincial curriculums we are now using can be carried through to provide the framework for reporting information, and the new assessment codes - levels, for example - can be used too when they have been properly explained and 'bedded down' so that they actually mean something. But if all this is attempted too often, or in too much detail, parents can be overwhelmed and teachers can be exhausted.

Involving Students Successfully, in Feedback and Feedforward

If we wish to involve learners actively in reflecting upon and correcting their own work, we may also have to consider their level of involvement in other parts of the learning process. Do we encourage our students to consider what they already know about a topic before treating it as 'new work'? Do we offer any choice of tasks? Do we allow the students to consider the assessment criteria, even if the assessment is actually done by the teacher? If the students have the criteria, could they help us design the task? These are not solutions, they are possibilities, to pull the students into a greater sense of involvement in and responsibility for their own learning. It's asking a lot of the students to expect active involvement immediately after a teaching process which may have encouraged passivity up to that point. It's also unrealistic to make such demands when the students reach their mid-teens, after they've got used to 'gliding through'.

If student involvement in learning is going to work it has to start when they're young, be carefully structured and nurtured as a developing skill and sustained as they get older. Only they, after all, can improve their learning ; teachers can only improve their teaching.

Key Points

1. Good feedback needs to be specific, timely, useful and used.

2. Words as well as codes are essential in feedback for improvement.

3. Different audiences need different kinds of feedback, despite the urge to find one method that suits everyone.

One big question

How do we encourage all learners to compete against their own previous best performance rather than just against each other?

Chapter Three:
Feedforward

The fifth of our big questions about assessment is 'So What?'. It makes so much sense to look forward and translate what we have learned into next steps to improve learning, but before we examine how best to do so, a brief tour of the potential potholes might prove salutory.

Setting targets can be very valuable. It provides a clear sense of direction for learning; it allows individual goals to be articulated and shared, so that others may support their pursuit; it enables progress to be measured over time with reference to the goals which have been set. But there's a down-side too. The target may inhibit growth if the target is set too low, or lead to complacency or cynicism when it is met with little effort: being specific in the face of an uncertain future may reduce our flexibility in adapting to changing circumstances, stemming from a misguided assumption of predictability, and in turn this may lead to the chance of explicit failure to achieve the pre-specified goal, with reduced motivation as a result. Behind this apparently benign process lurk some very real difficulties if target-setting is not treated with care: it may even make matters worse not better.

> *Question: Is it better to set ambitious targets and run the risk of failing to meet them, or set targets which reflect very little advance on your current position and meet them every time?*

> *Answer: No risk, no learning.*

> *Alternative answer: It depends how high the stakes are.*

In this chapter we're going to look first at the characteristics of effective targets, and then at the characteristics of effective target-setters. Finally I want to refer briefly to the idea of 'bench-marking' recently introduced in England and Wales, which may spread to other systems which are adopting numerical ways of describing learning as students move through school.

So what are the characteristics of effective targets? I'm not keen on acronyms – too trite to be useful much of the time – but in this case I make an exception. Let's hear it for SMART targets! The word itself is a good one – so long as you use the American definition of 'smart' meaning 'sharp and bright and clever', not the British one of 'tidy and well-presented' – something definitely lost in translation there.

More important is what the letters actually stand for.

SMART = Specific, Measurable, Achievable, Relevant, Time-Related

S is for Specific

We know about this. Vague targets are not much use really as nobody really knows what they mean, or how to achieve them, or what it would look like if they were achieved. Hardly worth having really, although vague targets are easy and undemanding. Specific targets, on the other hand, can be quite scary. They're clear and mistakeable, offering no place to hide when you come to check them out: no fudging, no escape. Specificity about the future is particularly worrying, because it carries that 'assumption of predictability' I mentioned before. All that we have learned in the 1990's about the perils of prediction, and we're still trying to say what we want the future to look like. But what else can you do? Unpredictable or not, the future will arrive, and setting targets for our future is still for me a perfectly reasonable human activity. Michael Fullan urges us to have faith – 'optimism without cause' – and I can see the value in that, and the perils of the alternatives. So we set specific targets, but not too far ahead, to reduce the risk of chaos intervening.

Sometimes perhaps the lack of specificity is not in our heads, but in what we choose to write down. In that case the best person to check that targets are specific enough is not yourself, but someone else. 'What do you mean by that?' is a useful question, prompting the other person to re-frame their thoughts, or add some more detail, and in doing so to become a little clearer herself. The act of target-setting, essentially, is a public rather than a private act. By bringing targets into the public domain we become publicly accountable for them: maybe that is both the worth of the exercise and one of the reasons why we may resist the need to be specific.

M is for **Measurable**

Obviously measureability is connected with specificity – if you don't really know what the target means how will you set out to find evidence of it. The idea of 'measurement' also smacks of numbers and quantification, and is perhaps not the best word to use – although it has the great advantage of beginning with M! We will need to define 'measurable' as 'able to be found or checked by a reasonably simple process'. 'Investigateable' is a word which sums it up for me, although the computer spell check rejects it every time.

The important need is to recognise that targets will be checked up on, and that there will be a way of determining whether they have been achieved, or not, or to what degree.

> When I work with teachers about setting targets for improving their own teaching, they sometimes tell me that their target is to make their students better motivated, or happier, or more effective learners. These are very worthy ambitions, but a nightmare to 'measure'. To check these properly, someone will need to pay very close attention to the reactions and perceptions of the students. I sincerely hope that this would happen, but the time and effort to do

it may mean that either the most subjective impression is taken as evidence or the task is rejected altogether as 'too hard'. Either way, the target may prove to be 'uncheckable', and therefore of little use. This sounds really dismissive of some of our finest teaching ambitions, which I regret: but I regret even more the potential of personal target-setting to generate improvement being undermined by our failure to think through the realities of investigating these targets at a later date.

When we set our targets, therefore, we should consider what evidence we might expect for their achievement, and how such evidence might be discovered, and by whom. Thinking back to those key assessment questions: in order to assess the achievement of our targets we have first to know what we're looking for, and that needs to be considered while the target is being defined, not forgotten until the need is upon us.

A is for **Achievable**

The targets for any of us as learners, adult or child, need to be **'within our extended grasp'**. A simple phrase but fundamentally important for teachers with their students and for any learner considering his or her next steps. If the target is too close to where we stand now, then there is no learning, or not as much as there needs to be. If the target is beyond our extended grasp, then we are faced with failure, not a problem occasionally, but a real problem if that failure is continual and unrelieved. In order to establish what is within or beyond this extended grasp we need really good information about both our starting point, and the nature of the task we have ahead of us. To establish achievable targets, learners need good specific feedback about their current learning. They also need to understand enough about the learning which may lie ahead of them to gauge what they still have to do, and how best to calibrate the stages in between. Poor information about present learning and future challenges will lead to poor target-setting: **feedback and feedforward are interdependent.**

In the early days of 'Recording Achievement' in some of
our schools, valiant efforts were made to encourage students
to set targets for their learning. Their early efforts were
often disappointing: 'I must try harder'. 'I must pay more
attention in Geography.' Teachers who were unsure about
target-setting, and who resented the time it took away
from what they considered to be real teaching, were now
convinced that the students simply couldn't do it: 'Our
students are just not mature enough to set targets for their
own learning', said a Sixth Form College teacher to me
with great confidence after recounting the students' efforts
to do so. Some discussion then ensued, among the rest of
the staff, about whether this was about some Piagetian
notion of 'readiness' or just that the students had received
no guidance in how to set effective targets, and that many
of them had no real idea of where their strengths and
weaknesses lay. 'If we tell them that grades are important,
but don't tell them what the grades actually require, then

how can we expect them to know what to do next?', was another teacher's contribution. Not for the first time I was struck by the fact that these teachers, who taught the same students, had never previously discussed their assumptions and expectations with each other, and were inevitably giving their students some very mixed messages about learning.

In the busy environment of school, achievable targets in one area have to be managed alongside a host of other things. Achieveability, therefore, is not just about the single task, but about the other tasks we have to handle simultaneously. Prioritising will help of course, but none of us have the luxury of being able to give all our attention to only one thing at a time.

R is for **Relevant**

Why on earth would anyone choose a target which is irrelevant? The most obvious answer to this question, considering all we've already established about the difficulties of choosing useful targets, is that the learner simply does not know what is relevant and what is not. If learners lack knowledge of their own learning, or have no idea what may be required of them to improve, then target-setting is bound to be 'hit and miss'. Under pressure to set targets, 'because that's what the teachers say we have to do', and confused about what that really means, many learners will just... 'pick a target, any target, the one I chose last term seemed to be OK so I'll try that one again, it won't matter anyway because we won't have to bother about them again'.

Another reason for choosing a target which may be irrelevant to the learner's next steps is that a relevant target is just too difficult either to identify or to attain. If you don't feel able to make progress towards what you need to learn, but do feel confident about the future in a different area, then there's a strong temptation to choose a target where there's more likelihood of success, and just hope that no-one notices that it's not really relevant.

To help people – either students or teachers, or anyone else come to that – establish relevant targets, I encourage them sometimes to visualise what it would look like if the future learning they're aspiring to were actually achieved. 'What will it look like when it's finished?' is a useful question sometimes. If you can see even the broad outline of the desired future, then you stay within that frame to find a next step which would help you towards it. Your choice may not be the one step which is at the heart of everything that needs to happen: that's asking too much, and anyway your choice will be affected by other considerations, but at least it'll be relevant to taking you where you want to go.

When considering changes in the school's assessment process, teachers often decide to involve their students more. To help focus on what that will mean in practice, I often ask them to envisage and describe the picture of a classroom in which the students are effectively involved in the assessment process. What can they see in their mind's eye? All sorts of detail comes out of this image of a future reality: the students will understand the strengths of their own work; they will occasionally be asked to assess their own or each others' work; they will be able to set useful and specific targets for improvement; they may be involved in selecting, annotating and managing samples of their own work to share with their parents, or the next teacher or school, or 'gatekeeper' for the next stage in their education, or a prospective employer. With a clearer picture of what we're aiming for, it's easier to decide what will need to be done to enable this specific future to happen.

One more thing about relevance before we move on. If one has absolute faith that learners alone know what they really need, and that their learning path might look impossibly rocky and meandering to someone else, then one would also have to accept the learner's targets without question. I can see this argument, but I don't agree with it, or at least not with most learning, most of the time. If someone presented to me learning targets which appeared to have nothing whatever to do with what I understood to be their next challenge, I would certainly want to ask about them, rather than just accept them. As the person's 'critical friend' my role is to 'gently challenge', but I could always accept the reasons for the learner's choice. There's bound to be disagreement about such a stance. What do you think? Would it make any difference to you if the learner was an adult rather than a child?

T is for **Time-related**

This is very closely connected to the need for targets to be achievable. All learning and development needs time for it to happen. A learning target which would be within your extended grasp over six weeks could be impossible if you give yourself only six days. When establishing a time-frame in which to achieve specific things, the need is for a balance of optimism and realism. If this particular target was all we had to deal with over the coming month then of course we could manage it, but it's not the only thing we have to deal with. Other things, of equal significance and importance, will have to be managed simultaneously. Some of these other things we can predict: other priorities may emerge of which we have no inkling at present.

A focus on realistic but still challenging time frames is essential for target-setting: sometimes school development plans have an air of unreality because they seem to assume that everything will work out as expected, and leave no room for mistakes, or delays beyond our control, or arguments which need time to be resolved. That's one reason for including in your development planning structure the need to estimate the cost of your proposed development not only in money but also in time – a scarce and finite resource in schools, unless you wish to overload people to the point of making them ineffective.

Writing about planning for students' learning (Assessment for Learning, Chapter 1), I urge teachers, even when they're trying to deal with the pressure of a required external curriculum, to leave some space within their plans for dealing with the unexpected, for consolidation, remediation and extension, and for periodic review of what's been achieved and where next. That same principle would apply here too. In establishing targets for learning and development, estimate the time you think it will take you to achieve the target, than add 10%. It may make the target look less impressive, but it will make a big difference to your chance of success.

Acronyms should be useful as well as memorable: I think SMART works well in both respects. I just wish we could work another letter in somewhere which represents the need for limiting the **number** of targets, as well as their individual characteristics. However finely-tuned each of your targets might be, if there are just too many of them all of them are at risk. It's the old spinning plates problem: add one plate too many and they all tumble. One or two targets actually achieved is probably more valuable than several unattained, abandoned or forgotten about, but here again it depends on your willingness to prioritise. Doing less better is risky, especially when your main concern is to survive external pressure to do everything at once.

Practice Makes it Better

Target-setting is a learned skill: it improves with practice. When I'm working with teachers we often take a little while at the end of the day or the programme to reflect on what we've been considering and decide next steps. I ask people to set themselves some targets, and write them down. Then I ask them to share their targets with one other person. For just a few minutes each way, each partner 'gently challenges' the other about their targets, and whether they are really SMART. Each person asks a few probing open questions of the other: 'What do you mean by that? Are you sure you can achieve that by then? How will you, or someone else, check that you have achieved this?' After just a few minutes conversation I ask everyone then to re-draft their targets, to make them SMARTer if necessary, or just to reduce the number of things they've set themselves to do. What a difference it makes. The questions have created a feedback loop, and feedback improves learning, in target-setting as in everything else.

Pre-conditions for Effective Target-setting

1. Recognition that it is a skill which is learnable, and which therefore can be taught, and the earlier in the learner's life, the better.

2. Useful specific information, about current learning strengths to be built upon and difficulties to be tackled. Such information can be generated through good assessment and feedback.

3. A clear view of what we are trying to achieve.

4. Encouragement and confidence to stretch beyond the known limits of current achievement; to take a risk, without fear of blame if the extended grasp is just not enough to reach the target. The 'learning culture', if we can call it that, accepts occasional failure as a part of learning, to be learned from. Such a culture must be in the staffroom as well as the classroom if teachers are truly to stretch themselves and support students to do the same.

Bench-marking: Target-setting for the School

School improvement runs the risk of becoming 'an initiative' (or 'yet another initiative') when it must of course be the continual aim of every school. Recently, the emphasis on quantifying the outcomes of learning through test and exam results expressed as levels and grades has provided a possible mechanism for the statistical measurement of school improvement, and the opportunity has been seized with alacrity by policy makers.

'Value-added' analysis is now the order of the day, and schools are encouraged to gather and analyse the available data to indicate the difference they have made to the learning of cohorts of their students as they progress through the school. 'League tables' in which all schools are arranged in an order of merit derived from raw results alone do not really hit the spot at all, quite apart from the confusion they present to many parents and the injustice to many schools. What is needed is a way of recognising some of the key variables which markedly affect performance and which lie beyond the control of the school. Then comparisons with like schools will reveal the strengths and weaknesses and provide clues about the necessary focus to improve the students' performance. Schools need also to find a way of assembling 'before and after' pictures of their students' achievements.

After struggling with these issues for some years, the Department for Education and Employment in the UK drew up proposals in 1996. Two important and measurable variables were identified as having an impact on school 'performance' the proportion of students entitled to a free school meal (a frequently used socio-economic indicator), and the proportion of students whose first language is not English. On the basis of this data schools are grouped into broad bands with like schools. Then the 'results' – examination grades and National Curriculum assessment levels – are published for each of the schools, so that they can be compared with each other, as a means for each school to analyse its strengths and needs. Schools are then encouraged to set themselves targets for the improved performance of cohorts of students by the end of the next stage in their schooling. These targets have to be shared with the school's governing body, and with the Office for Standards in Education (OFSTED) which is responsible for school inspection, making it both public and high stake, as both bodies are expected to call the school to account for the achievement or non-achievement of the stated targets. This process of comparison and target-setting has been given the title of 'bench-marking'.

A host of questions emerge from this development – really good questions which will 'focus the mind wonderfully'. (This was the phrase used by Dr Johnson in the 18th century to describe the effect of the threat of imminent execution.)

- Should schools aim for the norm within their 'band' of schools, or at an overall improvement percentage, or should they derive the improvement targets from very close analysis of their current performance followed by SMART target-setting from that starting point?

- Will schools be expected to improve at a uniform rate year after year, and what then happens when the achievement curve begins to flatten out?

- Should the teacher's predictions of future performance be shared with the students, or is bench-marking about cohort rather than individual performance?

I was working with a secondary school about disaggregating their GCSE results, to examine the specific performance of different students, and groups of students, so that they could make more informed predictions about their future learning, and ways of improving the performance of the next GCSE cohort. Some of the teachers had interpreted the need to work from disaggregated data towards aggregated targets as meaning that they should predict the GCSE performance of each student at the beginning of Year 10 and then tell the students and their parents what they were going to achieve. An argument ensued about whether or not this was a good idea. Would it achieve the desired result, which was an improvement in the students' grades? On the one hand, for some students a predicted grade so far ahead of the event might provide them with a real target to aim at, but only as long as they knew what the grade entailed, and how they might tackle steps towards its achievement. For other students the predicted grade might place a ceiling on their efforts, and inhibit them achieving what they might achieve with an all-out effort. Other students might be really de-motivated by the prospect of a result too poor to be of use to them, and give up prematurely. Some of the staff were unhappy at the prospect of identifying potential performance so far in advance, because of the impact it might have on their own motivation and effort as well as those of the students. They also worried about being blamed if a student subsequently failed to achieve what had been predicted for them.

Their preferred option in the end was to use such individual predictions to arrive at the baseline for their efforts to improve overall GCSE performance, but not to share these predictions with individual students. Instead they decided to revise their approach to marking and feedback in Years 10 and 11, making it much more explicit and related to the specific expectations for GCSE grades in each subject. The student would receive two types of feedback: one code or comment would relate to the effort and progress demonstrated within the student's performance; the other would indicate what grade level the performance would merit by GCSE standards, and why, and one or two next steps towards the next grade.

Their intention was to spend more time reviewing these grades and comments when work was returned, to ensure that they were understood and that students could keep track of their own progress towards identifiable and relevant goals. Target-setting for the students therefore was shorter term than target-setting for 'bench-marking' purposes.

- What about the tendency in some schools to regard some cohorts of students as 'a bad year'? Would this then mean that the targets for such a year were reduced, because the teachers believe that the habit of under-achievement is too ingrained to be set aside?

I have real trouble with the notion of a 'bad year' although it is not uncommon to hear teachers and school leaders talk about the phenomenon as if it were just a fact of life, about which very little could be done. Just as teachers sometimes consider their students as members of a particular group or class and categorise them as such, whole year groups of students can develop a sort of collective identity and members of that year group absorb the collective label. This label can be positive of course, and sometimes is, creating a shared positive expectation and self-image among the students which can be very beneficial for them. The negative collective label – the 'bad year' – is potentially very damaging both for the individual students who share it and for the expectations of those who teach them. It's the 'Horns and Halo Effect' writ large, and needs to be looked at very carefully. 'Disaggregated thinking' is needed here to pick apart this generic impression and see how it has arisen. If on reflection it appears that the achievement of the majority of the students is below what would normally be expected at their age and stage, then further enquiries

will be needed to determine why this is so, and what can be done about it. On the other hand, analysis of what makes it 'a bad year' may reveal the majority of students doing fine, but their success being hidden behind, or even undermined by, the poor performance of a small number of their peers, in which case quite a different course of action may be needed. In either case, intervention should have happened earlier, before the collective label had hardened into something which seemed impossible to change.

Perhaps the labelling and fatalism inherent in the concept of the 'bad year' can be consigned to the bin and we can begin to establish a sense of positive group identity for cohorts of students while still recognising each of them as individual learners.

- Do all schools have the skill and confidence needed to manage and analyse statistical data, and if not, where and how do they develop them?

I asked this question of a primary school coming to terms with the demands of bench-marking: the Head recognised that she didn't have the skills required, but one of the newly qualified teachers on the staff had had statistical experience in her previous job. It was agreed that this teacher should offer some advice and training to the rest of the staff, and give the Head some individual tuition too, so that she could develop her own skills.

- Is it sufficient to use only quantifiable data as the pointers to further enquiry: should schools pay equal attention to qualitative indicators of learning as a means of accelerating improvement, such as students' motivation, relationships in the classroom and parental perceptions?

Learning is a complex business, difficult to develop or to measure through only one set of strategies. For reasons I tried to explain in the Preface, we are expected in the

*current climate to try to quantify everything, which enables
the presentation of complex information in statistical
form, but we know this is only part of the story. Quantitative
and qualitative evidence need to be balanced, despite the
fact that the qualitative – such as students responses to
planned questions about their learning – may take longer
and produce 'softer' results. There's a fuller discussion of
this issue in my book on 'School Self Review', pages 35 –
40.*

- Do we give more emphasis to improving on our own previous best performance, or to overtaking the performance of others?

Although bench-marking may be in its early days, with the details likely to be changed as it is tried out for the first time, it is already possible to suggest the characteristics of those schools who will become successful target-setters, based on evidence of their experience of effective development planning. This list is based on my own experience of watching schools involve themselves in these procedures over the past decade or so. It is therefore not definitive, but would be a place to start in reflecting on your own school's capability in this area.

Schools and management teams which are good at target-setting seem to have the following characteristics:

- clarity about the school's overall purpose and aspirations, expressed in intelligible language;

- good data about teaching, learning and achievement – disaggregated, relevant and useful, both quantitative and qualitative;

- confidence and some skills in the analysis of statistical data, or knowledge of where to find and how to deploy such skills;

- clarity about the available resources within a given time-frame, ie. time, energy, optimism and goodwill, as well as money;

- the ability and necessary courage to prioritise, take some calculated risks, and cope with a degree of uncertainty;

- willingness to use failure as a source of new learning, and avoidance of blame;

- awareness of what is within the 'extended grasp' of the school, its teachers and its students;

- a culture of SMART target-setting for all the school's learners, which means the teachers as well as the students;

- the patience to motivate and harness the collective intelligence of the whole school, and then the courage to take action with a consensus if unanimity is unattainable;

- 'Ready, Fire, Aim' rather than 'Ready, Aim, Fire': good judgement is needed about the timing of the first attempt to try something out. If you take too long to work out exactly how a process will work, you run the risk of talking yourselves to a standstill ('Ready, Ready, Ready'). There will come a time when you've thought and discussed enough, and the rest of your learning will need to come from 'having a go'. So you 'Fire', and use the experience to fine tune ('Aim') the detail of the strategy for the next attempt.

One term in this list needs a little more explanation - 'disaggregation'. I'm no mathematician, but I know that clumping information together into aggregated blobs is not the kind of information we need for close analysis of strengths and needs, for students, for teachers or for schools. If assessment is to be useful for planning improvement it must provide specific information about specific things. Data about results must be picked apart to tell us which aspects of which learning areas were achieved well and not so well by which students, in which classes. Within the disaggregated data we look for the clues we need to decide what to do. When we know which variables most affect results then we can make a start to improve things : without such understanding all we can do is try harder, work harder, do more, and much of our energy and resources will lack focus and be dissipated. Sometimes the outcomes of this unpicking of the data provide uncomfortable reading. It will be clear, for instance, that a particular teacher or team is not achieving the results produced by other teachers or teams, or that some aspects of our teaching are clearly less successful than others. But for every problem identified there will also be a success story, if we look for it. The feedback we provide for ourselves should have all the characteristics of effective feedback we identified in Chapter Two: then we can begin to set our targets with a clearer focus, and more chance of success.

Key Points

1. Good target-setting always involves an element of risk.

2. SMART target-setting is a learned skill and improves with practice.

3. Relevant, accurate, disaggregated information is an essential starting point for planning improvement.

One big question

What do you do when well-planned targets are not achieved?

Chapter Four:
Teacher Appraisal: Why? What? Who? How?

This book is about 'The Learning School'. It is based on the premise that learning requires a constant flow of useful information about what we want or need to achieve, how we're getting on and what needs to be done next to pursue our learning goals. Much of the focus so far, in this book and in many others about student and school improvement, has been on the assessment of students' learning, feedback and feedforward. Now I want to present a further premise which lies for me at the centre of the idea of the 'Learning School': teachers are learners too, and everything we believe about assessment, feedback and feedforward should and can be applied to teachers as well as their students.

I am quite certain that in times past teachers have not regarded themselves, or been regarded by others, as learners. The teacher historically has been an authority figure, guardian of truth and wisdom to be imparted to the next generation: the 'domine' was exactly that, the 'master' of the learning environment not a participant in it. To suggest otherwise could be damaging to that very authority which teachers so valued, as it might suggest that teachers still had things to learn, and that they could make mistakes, and be unworthy of the respect they needed from their students, and their parents, and the community at large.

That was then and this is now. Teachers still need and want respect from their students and the community but the basis of such respect has changed, as so much else in our society has changed over the past half century. A number of factors combine which persuade us to review the role of the teacher. The late twentieth century has seen an increasing assertion of the legal rights and entitlements of children: they can no longer, for example, be physically punished in schools, and are encouraged more than ever before to stand up for themselves, at school and beyond. Many teachers, past and present, applaud this recognition of children's rights, but without doubt it has altered the power relationship between teachers and taught. The knowledge expertise which distinguished teachers from their students is also eroding already, and will erode further, as the knowledge base expands and students can use access to technology as a resource not controlled by the teacher or the school. The technology itself can even be seen to make the child more powerful than the adult, as my generation struggles to come to terms with its needs and implications and finds a six-year old to programme the video.

> *A friend of mine was discussing with her grandson Michael's teacher his imminent transfer to secondary school at the age of eleven. After some reference to the child's needs, the teacher said, 'I'm just not sure what we're going to do when he leaves.' 'I'm sure the soccer team will manage fine without him,' said my friend. 'Oh yes,' said the teacher, 'it's not the soccer team we're worried about. You see, Michael's been looking after all our school computers for the past two years. If anything goes wrong we always send for him first. Now we'll have to find another child to do it, because none of us knows how, and it'll cost a fortune to buy in help from outside.' 'There's still time,' said my friend, 'you'll have to get Michael to take the teachers through the systems and give you all some coaching before he leaves.'*

This is not the place to explore all these issues in depth. Suffice to say that for a variety of reasons and in a variety of ways teachers now need to learn more during the course of their careers than they may have needed to before. My hope is also that teachers **want** to learn more, for more than merely instrumental reasons.

If you yourself are bored, can you avoid being boring? If you yourself only ever respond to extrinsic motivation to learn, can you offer to your students any notion of the intrinsic worth of involvement in learning?

We need to make the assumption that most if not all teachers believe they are still learning, about teaching, about their subject or specialism, about new skills or about themselves. Some of this learning may not be related to their job, but much of it will be. Even if the evidence of the product of learning might not be visible daily in school, we could expect that evidence of the process of learning might have an impact on the way we teach. Assessment, feedback and feedforward are part of learning : how do we make this happen for teachers as learners.

In this chapter I'm going to apply to teachers as learners the three big ideas, and five questions we looked at in Chapter One, and see what light this may shed on the process variously described as Teachers Appraisal, or Performance Management, or Performance Review, or whatever. No doubt someone agonises over these titles : is this because the choice of words symbolises something about the purpose? Before examining the first big question – Why? – let's review the first idea, that assessment is integral to learning, and to teacher development.

"There is no learning without some difficulty and fumbling.

If you want to keep on learning, you must go on risking failure - all you life. It's as simple as that."

(author unknown)

Found on the staff room door at
Kaingaroa School, New Zealand

Here again is the diagram representing the cycle of learning and assessment :

The Cycle of Teaching, Assessment and Development

Intentions for teaching and development

Analysing outcomes

Managing learning and development

Reporting appropriate information

Gathering information about learning and development

Recording significant outcomes

- All parts of the cycle need to be consistent with each other
- The cycle is complete only when information is 'fed forward' into planning and management of learning
- 'Assessment' described here as 'observing the outcomes of learning' is integral to teaching
- Assesment promotes learning through specific feedback to the learner

Look at it again from the point of view of the teacher as learner. The teacher has intentions for his own learning and development, which come from within himself or in response to external needs and requirements. He seeks out, creates, or is offered tasks which enable him to learn what he intends to learn. Then he — or someone else — gathers information about whether his learning aims have been achieved, and to what degree. Not wishing to rely on memory alone, significant information about learning is recorded somewhere, somehow by someone. Using this information, feedback is offered to the teacher, and targets set for the future, to build on what has been achieved and tackle what has not. These targets will come from analysis of learning outcomes to date, and will in turn affect the teacher's future plans, so that opportunities for new learning can be found and used. The targets too will be recorded somewhere and become the basis for assessment of future learning. And so it goes on. The cycle stops only when there is nothing more to learn.

Already we've made certain assumptions about the purpose of Teacher Appraisal: now's the time to apply the five assessment questions, starting with Why?

Why assess teachers? Who is it for?

The reasons for assessing teachers can be divided into three main categories:

1. To develop skills and knowledge in any aspect of their individual professional activity and aspirations : for the individual teacher.

2. As an accountability check concerned with contractual duties and competency, and possibly with remuneration : for the management of the school, or whoever else officially 'employs' the teacher.

3. As a central part of a strategy for improving teaching and learning: for the school.

These three purposes overlap with each other, and at first glance it might seem sensible to merge them into one process. Early experience has seemed to show, however, that these purposes are best thought through, at least initially, as separate exercises, so I'll first explore them one at a time.

>*Purpose No.1*   Individual professional development is concerned only and entirely with the needs and support of the individual teacher. The focus for the appraisal, if any, is chosen by the individual teacher, who is then supported by someone else who will gather evidence of the outcomes of this focus, share them with the 'appraisee' and help her to plan further learning which will be supported wherever possible by the school through its staff development programme. There is a limited element of accountability, which has been described as 'holding oneself to account in the presence of another professional'.
>
>The assessment process, therefore, is very much driven by the individual, with another person involved to support and clarify rather than to judge. The outcome of the process is known to the individual teacher and their appraisal 'partner' but not necessarily to anyone else, and confidentiality is an important concern. Targets for development, similarly, may be shared with the staff development organiser, but beyond that they remain personal to the appraisee.
>
>The relative 'privacy' of this process, and the very specific use to which assessment information may be put, make it relatively safe for the appraisee to be honest about their needs as well as their strengths, and face possibly unflattering feedback, because it cannot be used in any way which connects with his/her security of employment or remuneration. Appraisees may of course wish to share any of this information with others, but that is their choice and

not a requirement of the process. The purpose is personal professional growth, nothing more.

Purpose No.2 The contractual purpose produces quite a different process. The duties and responsibilities of the teacher are described quite specifically, and evidence of the successful, or at least satisfactory, conduct of these duties is sought by the appraiser, representing the interests of the employer. This will be checked regularly, almost as if the teacher was on a short-term contract which had to be renewed. Most likely, the check is made before any annual increment is awarded, such increments no longer being automatic. The checking process may vary from school to school, but the Principal or Headteacher has to validate it, acting as the employers' representative.

The focus of the appraisal may be determined by the individual teacher, or by negotiation, within the parameters of the specific role and responsibilities, but parts of it at least are likely to be non-negotiable. It is a high-stake process, having an impact on future salary and possibly on future employment, and as such is likely to be more bureaucratic, having fixed procedures for the gathering, judgement and use of evidence of competence, to protect the employers from being deceived and the teacher from being unfairly treated.

Because of the use to which assessment information will be put, the teacher is likely to want to avoid any unflattering or unfavourable information emerging from the appraisal, and may be tempted to 'put on a show' for the appraiser, presenting herself or himself as well as possible, for a while at least.

Purpose No.3 If the assessment of teachers is to be directly linked to school improvement but not necessarily to individual contracts and remuneration, a different set of procedures again will pertain. Here the guide to the choice of focus will not be the individual teacher's aspirations, or the letter of the job description, but the planned priorities of the school and the team of which the teacher is a part. These shared and collective priorities will be the area where evidence of performance is sought and subsequently shared with both the individual teacher and her colleagues who are engaged in similar activities with a similar focus. They will share their successes with a view to spreading best practice, and share their failures too, expecting to find support, ideas and further useful feedback from the group.

This is a more public process than the first of the three, and less high-stake than the second. Issues of confidentiality and privacy are relatively unimportant, the feedback is largely descriptive rather than evaluative, and the aim of the exercise is school improvement via the improvement of the teacher as part of a learning team.

The Importance of 'Fitness for Purpose' in Teacher Appraisal

Clearly, virtually no decisions can be made about how to assess teachers until the purpose of the exercise is agreed and transparent. The formal title of the process may give some clue as to its purpose, but is not enough on which to build. The rhetoric of most appraisal proposals will talk about what is in the best interests of the students, but that too is insufficient without a specific explanation of how these interests are to be best met. There will be argument and possibly disagreement about the means even if no-one disagrees about the ends, and such argument is necessary to achieve a degree of honesty and clarity which will encourage intelligent people to engage with the process.

> *In 'School Improvement – What can Pupils Tell Us?, (Fulton,1996) one of the authors, Gwen Wallace, describes her research team's efforts to establish, through interviews with secondary school students, the school and classroom*

*conditions which encourage students to become **'engaged'** with their learning. 'We use this term,' she says, 'because its meaning goes **beyond compliance** to denote a level of emotional involvement in school work.' Such involvement is the key factor in successful learning, whether the motivation which fuels this engagement is intrinsic (interest in the activities and their outcomes) or extrinsic (the need to get good grades as a means to the desired goal).*

Maybe the question about appraisal for school improvement should be, how can the process lead to the 'engagement' of teachers in their learning, using the same balance of intrinsic and extrinsic motivation which is present in the learning conditions we provide for younger learners?

Terry Crooks has described the need to consider the 'impact' of the assessment system we design, and check its efficacy by the degree to which the desired impact actually results. We could design an appraisal process on the same basis. 'Fitness for impact' should provide us with a similar blueprint as 'fitness for purpose', but the thinking process starts in a slightly different place. Another closely related way of considering the same issue would be to ask, in relation to your appraisal process, 'What will it look like when it's finished?', and design backwards from your specific vision of a future reality.

Can these three Appraisal purposes happen simultaneously?

Curiously, I feel the answer may be 'Yes', although I have not yet seen them do so.

The focus of the first national appraisal initiative in England and Wales, agreed through a working group of teachers' unions and government representatives (an unprecedented event in policy formation under the Conservative govenment), was very much the first model described above. Suspicions of the government's motives ran very deep — understandably, if you've read my impression of the context of educational change in the Preface of this book. Privacy, confidentiality and a focus on individual development were seen as the only ways of protecting teachers from these ulterior motives. Five years on, two successive evaluations revealed that the process was widely regarded as too time-consuming for its apparent ineffectiveness, and a review is currently (1997) underway to breathe life back into it.

Interestingly, in New Zealand, under a government of similar political hue, but five years after the original UK proposals, 'Performance Management ' for teachers was introduced with features more reminiscent of the second model on our list above than either of the other two, and then incorporated into newly agreed contracts with the two teachers' associations, as part of the price for improved pay and conditions. It will be interesting to see whether the impact of this system on teachers and school managers is 'compliance' or 'engagement'.

It should, in principle, be possible to pursue both contractual accountability and professional growth as simultaneous purposes of a school appraisal system, so long as the two do not overlap. If they do overlap, the high-stake nature of the one will tend to overturn the softer impact of the other, as teachers 'play safe' to protect themselves from the damaging consequences of identifying their professional weaknesses and needs as well as their strengths. That's a personal view, based on some experience and some evidence from other professions, but you may well disagree. What we believe about this does have a major bearing on all the other assessment choices we will face in designing an effective appraisal process.

Assessing Teachers: What?

After that fairly circuitous ramble around the issues of purpose, the question of what is to be assessed will already have had an implicit if not explicit airing. In the first of the three models outlined above – the 'individual growth' model – the areas to be assessed will be defined by the individual teacher. If she wants feedback on her classroom activities, that's what she will get. If on the other hand she's interested in her relationships with parents rather than the students, that's OK too.

In fact anything's OK, so long as it is related in some way to her professional responsibilities. To have any chance of success, as we have already seen, an assessment process must prioritise its focus, so some choice is essential, and in this case the choice is the teacher's. In the second scenario – the 'contractual accountability' model – the assessment foci are presumably closely connected with the teacher's contractual duties, but beyond that there may be choice negotiated. In the New Zealand model, the appraisee did have some choice, but assessment of classroom teaching was a requirement. In the third – the 'school improvement ' model, the assessment foci are derived directly from the development targets of the school and its sub-teams as reflected in their respective development plans, with choices if necessary made by the team rather than individuals.

In all three of these models we have to assume that teachers, individually or collectively, are clear what it is they are being asked to do. What do we mean by 'effective classroom teaching', or 'successful team leadership', or 'encouraging high standards' or any of the other worthy aspirations we articulate about our professional activities. In many schools no doubt, and for many teachers, the specific expectations which can be drawn from these expressions are quite clear, but there are also many schools where such matters have not been properly discussed for too long. Teachers are often expected to absorb professional expectations by some form of osmosis, and the discussion about them rarely gets beyond the level of generalities.

One of the most positive implications of any effective attempt to assess teachers and teaching is the necessary pre-requisite to define what we mean by 'good teaching' , in plain language with specific examples, so that everyone involved in the assessment process knows what they're aiming and looking for. If that pre-requisite is not met, there may be assessment but it will lack consistency and fairness and be to that extent unreliable. That is definitely not to say that all teachers must teach in the same way, but some shared principles about quality should underpin what we do, or the student's experience is largely a matter of which teachers they have. It is also frequently claimed that some of the most unorthodox teachers are the most successful, and therefore any parameters placed around our choice of teaching behaviours are unhelpful. Of course there will be the occasional highly idiosyncratic teaching genius who does not conform to any norms, however broadly they are defined. If they are wonderful teachers, for all their students not just a chosen few, leave them alone : the rest of us can still benefit from an explicit discussion of what makes a really good teacher.

> *In England and Wales, OFSTED, the school inspection agency, has produced guidelines about many aspects of school life for the use of its inspectors, and these have also been of great interest to schools. In its attempt to clarify the expectations about classroom teaching which would underpin its appraisal process, a secondary school took the OFSTED outline about the 'Quality of Teaching', and for each heading the teachers explored together what they thought would be the 'indicators' which could be sought in the classroom, or elsewhere, as evidence of this quality. The headings and questions they discussed were taken straight out of the OFSTED Handbook :*
>
> *1. Is the teaching purposeful?*
>
> *2. Does the teaching create and sustain interest and motivation?*
>
> *3. Does the teaching cater for the abilities and needs of all the pupils?*

4. *Are the expectations appropriate for all pupils?*

5. *Are lessons managed in ways that ensure an efficient and orderly approach to teaching and learning?*

6. *Is there effective interaction between teacher and pupils?*

7. *Is evaluation of pupils' progress used to support and encourage them, and to extend and challenge them appropriately?*

The staff, first in mixed subject groups and then sharing in the larger group, looked for clearly expressed 'indicators' for each of these areas in an attempt to ensure that the specific assessment criteria to be employed in the appraisal process were at least commonly understood. The discussion also prompted the sharing of assumptions and expectations among different subject teachers which rarely took place because of the large and fragmented nature of the school. (In a smaller primary or middle school there might be more frequent opportunities for sharing such specific expectations, but these opportunities may not be used.)

It didn't really matter where the original prompt to consider these issues came from, but using the OFSTED list had that nice balance of intrinsic and extrinsic motivation which encouraged teachers to 'engage' with the task.

Whatever the chosen focus for appraisal and feedback, some specific criteria or 'indicators' need to be established beforehand, to make sure that the teacher and the 'assessor' are both clear about the information to be gathered. It is only when they are clear what is to be checked that they can then decide who is best placed to do such checking, and by what methods.

Because the quality of classroom teaching needs to be the main focus of teacher appraisal, I want to add a little more about the evidence which can be connected with it. Teaching is a complex process, and measuring its effectiveness is not easy. One type of 'evidence' may tell part of the story, but not all of it. To establish more valid and reliable information in the assessment of teaching we will need to **'triangulate'**. Impressive stuff! Actually, it's quite a simple idea, borrowed from more sophisticated academic evaluation practice than we usually have time for in school. There are no prizes for guessing that 'triangulation' involves gathering information from three perspectives to establish a more rounded and accurate picture of a complex phenomenon. The picture will be more accurate than that which can be derived from lots of information from only once source, and this has a bearing on the issue of 'sufficiency' referred to in Chapter One.

Let me try to exemplify triangulation with respect to the assessment of teaching. Take the first question in the OFSTED list about the quality of teaching – 'Is the teaching purposeful?'. Indicators of this desired quality could be found in the teacher's plans, where one would expect to find clear objectives, and planned activities and assessment designed to pursue and check these objectives. Evidence of purpose could also be seen in the teacher's introduction of the tasks to his students, and the sharing with them of the objectives which are followed through into feedback. Finally, anyone looking for evidence of purpose as perceived by the students might need to talk to them about it, or include some questions about purpose in a range of other information to be gathered from them.

Here are the three types of evidence – teachers' plans; classroom presentation; and students' reactions. Any one of these would give part of the picture, but all three would provide much richer data, worthy of close analysis as the foundation for planned improvement in this aspect of teaching.

Who and How?

These questions, unfortunately, are often the first ones to be tackled when schools consider a teacher appraisal scheme:

unfortunate because they could save themselves time, and do a much better job by tackling the Why? and the What? first. When you do that, as I've just done, the answers to the first questions stray over in to the answers to these two. As someone said to me recently : 'Agree the purpose, and the rest of it just falls out.' Curious choice of words, but he was right — it does just 'fall out'.

Answers to the Who? question can be found among the range of people available to us. You can place these possibilities along a line which starts with the teacher herself and ends with the most 'external' person you can think of – an expert on teaching who's never met the teacher before – and then fill in the gaps between these two extremes. Closest to the teacher would be a colleague who is also a friend; then a colleague with whom there is a professional but not personal relationship; then the person the teacher is accountable to, such as a team leader; then the team leader's leader, and so on up the 'heirarchy' of the school; then an outsider connected to the school like a governor or a trustee, or a parent. Finally, we're back to the outside expert. And that's only the adults: we've already concluded that the students may be called upon to provide information about the teacher's achievement, even if a judgement is made by someone else. Choice of the most appropriate person from those possibilities will be made on the basis of the purpose of the exercise, and the evidence or 'indicators' to be checked.

In the 'individual development' model of appraisal, the teacher herself will play a major part, and she may even choose the person who will help her gather evidence and reach conclusions about it. She is unlikely to choose someone she doesn't know and trust, but she might. The teacher's choice would be affected by the area being investigated, but she would think all that through and make her decision and the school would do its best to accommodate her wishes.

The 'contractual accountability' model will have much more fixed procedures about who assesses whom, probably reflecting the lines of management accountability already established in the school, with an appeal process available where there is a gross lack of respect or trust between appraiser and appraisee.

The Principal will be appraised by her peers or those who employ her, and she in turn will appraise the Deputies, who will appraise the team leaders, and so on. As it involves pay and conditions, and is conducted on behalf of the employers, procedures will be clearly laid down and there will be minimal flexibility.

The 'school improvement' model hovers between the other two. There may be less freedom of choice because the founding premise is about people working in teams towards collective goals, and the appraiser might be chosen by negotiation between the appraisee and the school, rather than by the appraisee alone, depending on what was to be investigated. In hierarchical terms, this model is more neutral, being driven by issues rather than people.

Self-Appraisal

Self-assessment by the teacher, reflecting on his own skills, strengths, difficulties and needs will be part of any effective appraisal process, whichever system or model is adopted. After all the information is gathered, and the feedback received and the targets set, the only person who can ultimately improve his teaching is the teacher, not just on those occasions when someone else is watching, but day after day. Just as it is with students, self-assessment is a learned skill. Some people have an innate gift of quick and clear insight about their own skills, almost as if they were observing themselves from the outside, but most of us don't have such a gift. We need to learn how to do it and practice.

Some people too seem to have an in-built aversion to any form of introspection, personal or professional. It's not that they can't do it, they won't do it, and seem to believe that thinking and talking about their teaching is as impossible as thinking and talking about themselves as a person.

In my first year of teaching, working in a classroom separated from the clattering kitchens by a thin screen, and coping with more than my fair share of less-motivated adolescents (well that's my story anyway), I struggled and got despondent sometimes about whether I would ever be any good, about whether my students respected me, about all the things that many young teachers worry about. At the opposite end of the classroom from the clattering kitchen was another set of screens, beyond which was my neighbouring teacher, an ex-Navy man of iron discipline whose students seemed always to be quiet and respectful. His idea of being supportive to me was to heave back the screens which divided us from time to time, loom in the gap for a while while my students recovered from the shock and then point at an offender, with no reference to me. 'You boy,' he would hiss, 'in here, now.' The offender would slink next door for the remainder of the period, the screens would close, and I would attempt to continue, trying to control my embarrassment and to take advantage of the fear his presence had created. I am quite sure my neighbour's intentions were to help me: but I did not feel helped. His fatherly advice to me on these occasions, delivered from his considerable height, was that I must learn to leave myself at home, and spend the day acting the role of teacher. Only then would the innate cruelty of the students not touch me.

That's the way it worked for him. For me, then and now, that way of working doesn't appeal. Who I am and how I teach (adults these days, not young people) are too close to be artificially separated, and the price you pay is that the job does get to you sometimes. It's still a price worth paying. A friend of mine, a doctor, had a similar struggle between the need to create some kind of distance between

> *herself and her patients and the need to remain humanly*
> *capable of feeling, without which she couldn't function.*

Clumsily, I'm trying to clarify why it may be that some teachers find self-assessment so difficult. It's too personal and has to be marginalised. As a gross generalisation, more men seem to have trouble with this than women, and none of the men I've encountered who flatly refuse to reflect on their own achievement has been willing or able to say why they find it too hard, saying only that they won't do it, it's not their job. This is particularly true in very rule-driven school climates, or where relationships are very formal.

> *Training on these issues, you have to decide when to push*
> *for involvement and when to leave people alone. On one*
> *occasion I was asking teachers to work in pairs, talking*
> *about their positive achievements over the past year, and*
> *the things they wished they'd done differently, just to see*
> *what it felt like to talk in some detail to another person*
> *whom they might not know. Just as we started the session,*
> *after a break, two people came into the room slightly late.*
> *I greeted them warmly and explained the task to them.*
> *They looked slightly bemused and I decided to encourage*
> *them into it, told them how useful they'd find it, placed*
> *each of them with a partner they didn't know well, and off*
> *we went. Twenty minutes later, as the group began to*
> *share what they'd experienced and felt, one of these two*
> *raised his hand, said how much he and his colleague had*
> *enjoyed it, but they ought to leave now because they were*
> *from a double-glazing company and had just come in to*
> *check the windows.*

When attitudes are as various as this, and if some element of self-assessment must be part of a teacher appraisal process, then it's going to need some structure, to avoid the personal choices which some will find difficult. Those teachers who don't really need such scaffolding will probably not object to using it, and gradually the structure will loosen and be discarded as it becomes redundant, for those teachers at least. It is not difficult for teachers themselves to design a structure for reflection about teaching, to be used before the initial meeting with the appraiser. Here's one a school came up with to get them through the initial difficulties they were experiencing.

1. Which specific teaching activities have worked best for me this year? Why? What made them successful?

2. Which specific teaching activities have not worked so well? Why? What would have helped them work better?

3. Is there any pattern about what's working well and what isn't?

4. Are there any factors which seem to be preventing me from doing a better job? Any suggestions about overcoming any of these?

5. One or two things I'd like to focus on next year, relevant to the classroom and any other aspect of my job.

Your school may well have something similar to or more effective than this. If it works, use it. A simple framework like this just prompts thinking, and adds structure to the first conversation with the appraiser, if you need a structure. It's clearly work-related, rather than something more personal, but is open-ended enough to allow someone to think more deeply if they wish.

Deciding the Method of Information Gathering

In choosing the methods to be used, here again a range of options is available. If the evidence being sought is on paper – the teacher's plans or record book, or samples of the students' work – the agreed person gathers and scrutinises it, probably with a focus or checklist of characteristics, just as if they were 'marking' a student's assignment. Asking questions of people on the receiving end of the teacher's professional activity is another method commonly used, and could mean arranging to talk to some students, or parents, or co-workers on a team or a project within school or outside. If there is a choice of who to talk to, who makes that choice, and who decides the questions to be asked? Decisions on these questions will go back to earlier ones, particularly to the purpose of the exercise. If a key purpose is for the teacher to receive worthwhile feedback and be motivated to improve her teaching, what procedures do you believe would best achieve that purpose? What 'impact' do you want this process to have, and how will that impact best be realised?

The planning process I'm describing here sounds cumbersome written down like this, and there's a strong temptation sometimes to say to schools 'Just use your common sense to decide what's best', but experience tells me that in the area of teacher appraisal common sense is not always enough, because it can be obscured by anxiety, fear, power-tripping, and sundry other attitudes. Teaching has been for so long and for so many the second most private human activity, that suggestions that it can and should be 'assessed' raise fears which may take a while to allay. As we shall discuss later, after a year or two when the process has been tried and is more trusted, then some of the careful thinking required to start with will feel more like 'common sense'. But in the early stages, anxieties are real and need to be respected, and the structure of planning suggested here provides the 'scaffolding' on which clear and defensible procedures can be built.

Balancing Validity, Reliability, Manageability, Cost and Public Acceptability in Teacher Appraisal

In Chapter One we explored this permanent dilemma of educational assessment in some depth, using the assessment of students as the main context. Now I want to apply these ideas to the assessment of teachers, to see how this might illuminate some of the choices we need to make. Here again I'll take the components of the dilemma one at a time.

Validity

In teacher appraisal this will require that :

1. information gathered about teaching relates very closely to the definitions and objectives of high quality teaching adopted by the school. If no clear agreement exists about this, validity may occur by accident, but not by design;

2. teachers being assessed should be offered a proper opportunity to 'show what they know and can do';

3. sufficient relevant information is available for a valid conclusion to be reached.

Therefore: the practical implications of these requirements are, for example, that information gathered about the teacher's teaching should be based on more than a few minutes' classroom observation; and that the information should be central to the agreed teaching objectives, and use methods appropriate to the observation of outcomes related to those objectives.

> *The teacher who spoke to me privately about her appraisal experience at the end of a workshop was frustrated, and now she knew why. 'We'd agreed that the main focus for my appraisal was matching activities to the students' learning pace and style', she told me, 'but then he [the appraiser] went on a course about classroom interaction and got really excited about it. He came into my room with a clipboard and a stop watch and started drawing diagrams. At the end of the session he wanted to show me this stuff, and it was quite interesting, but it didn't have much to do with the focus we'd agreed. He said it was more 'objective' than finding out whether the students were doing*

> *appropriate work, that he didn't have any more time to come to my classroom again, and that was all I was going to get. I suppose I can use what he gave me to think about classroom interaction, but it wasn't my priority, and I think he should have told me beforehand.'*

Reliability

To be reliable (or at least reliable enough), teacher appraisal will need to:

1. ensure that people making judgements about the quality of teaching are using consistent interpretations of the agreed definitions of 'quality' rather than highly personal or idiosyncratic expectations;

2. consider the 'typicality' of the teaching or other evidence of achievement they gather, to reduce irrelevant contextual variables. It would be inappropriate, for example, to observe someone teaching when they were clearly not well, or in other extraordinary circumstances, unless a further opportunity was planned in more normal circumstances later. Information about the teacher's ability to manage in extraordinary circumstances might be illuminating, but not as evidence of the agreed substantive focus.

As is also the case with the assessment of students, the higher the 'stake' of the assessment, the more emphasis is placed on the reliability of the process. Assessment for improvement tends to focus more on validity. The issue of reliability therefore will be central to teachers' perception of 'fairness' when promotion or pay may be determined at least in part as a result of the appraisal process.

> *In New Zealand where relatively high-stake 'performance management' has been built into teachers' and Principals'*

contracts, the teachers associations will be pressing for clear agreed procedures to ensure their members are treated fairly by the process, and the school Trustees, who are legally the teachers' employers, will be equally insistent on proper legally defensible procedures to be followed to protect them from accusations of bias in the conduct of their employment duties. The Principal of the school stands in the middle, also keen to avoid legal or other difficulties, but wishing simultaneously to preserve an honest and productive approach to the analysis and improvement of teaching and learning in the school. Quite an elaborate gavotte could result, until precedents are set and some degree of trust in the process is established.

Manageability and Cost

An effective and purposeful appraisal process is not cheap, but careful planning can certainly make it more cost-effective than some of the systems I have seen in operation. The main scarce and costly resource which has to be managed is **time**. Before the actual mechanics of an appraisal system are costed, thinking and planning time needs to be invested, in the hope that the investment will be rewarded – which it almost always is in my experience. On behalf of the school someone needs to do some homework – reading a book like this for example, thinking about and discussing the right questions in the right order. There will come a point at which you've thought enough and need to move on, to draft some proposals and plan a 'dry run' which will help to expose the unanticipated fish-hooks. That first experience will be evaluated, and the findings used to improve the process for the first whole-school attempt at implementation.

From the beginning of the 'homework/research' stage to the completion of the first whole-school pilot could be accomplished within a year, or maybe slightly longer, depending on the size of the school, the layers of agreement which will need to be reached and so on. This may sound like a long time, but some of the issues can be quite tricky, especially when there is little prior experience in the school, or relationships are not good in some areas. If you rush, the disagreements and unresolved questions will probably slow you down later, so take it quite slowly, spreading the base of decision-making and checking as you go.

At the implementation stage, begin to calculate the time requirements, bearing in mind that the first attempts at any new system usually take longer (like a dress rehearsal) and the process speeds up with familiarity and practice. There will be time needed to arrange for the information about the agreed focus areas to be gathered, and then time for actual gathering – through classroom observation, or interviews, or checking plans or whatever methods are agreed. Then there's time needed for review of the information, drawing conclusions, writing statements and setting targets. The targets may not be checked formally until the cycle begins again, probably in the following year, but before then there will probably be the need for a 'progress check'.

Let's count minutes.

At the very beginning, before the details of any individual appraisals are addressed, everyone who is going to be involved needs some basic preliminary information, a chance to discuss the implications, and some skill-building about classroom observation, giving and receiving effective feedback, and target-setting. With some careful planning, you could achieve this in a 'teacher-only' day. Such training, by the way, needs to be offered to everyone, whether or not they will be an appraiser as well as appraisee in the first round.

The pre-assessment meeting to arrange the focus and how the information is to be gathered would probably take 30 minutes or so, assuming that both parties were pretty well-informed about what they needed to do and about the rationale for the whole exercise.

The gathering of information will be more efficient and more effective if you can:

- involve the teacher;

- prioritise and choose a small number of important focus areas;

- sample evidence within a focus area rather than try to examine everything.

Classroom observation should be given sufficient time for the teacher to be seen properly at work : random 'popping in' is easy, but really not good enough. There isn't sufficient information to build sound conclusions and targets on. In a secondary school, one class period would be a minimum; in the primary school, about the same length of time. This may seem like a major time investment, but is a minute fraction of the time the students are with that teacher. If classroom teaching and learning are the key to school improvement, then you can't skimp this one. The important thing is to ensure that the hour or so is well-planned, the observer has some training, gathers descriptive rather than evaluative feedback, and then uses it effectively to support planned improvement.

Feedback, 'reports' and target-setting should be done at one go, within days of gathering the information, and completed within, probably, 30-50 minutes. If the groundrules for giving and receiving feedback have been agreed beforehand, the 'report' takes the form of a pro-forma (to be completed by agreement at the end of the discussion), and you're clear how to set SMART targets, it can be quite a smooth and well-organised event. It all depends how much time and care has been invested previously to make it so. In the following chapter these issues are discussed in greater detail.

As a brief summary: questions of validity are best addressed in the pre-planning, – first of the procedures themselves, and then of the information gathering process once you've agreed the focus areas. Reliability concerns can be addressed in the planning too, with some good whole-school discussion about what you're all looking for, allaying as far as possible the anxieties about purpose and fairness. With good investment of time at the planning stages, the time needed for implementation can be reduced without loss of quality. Exactly the same can be said about any assessment process.

Public Acceptability

This might more accurately read 'Political Acceptability' as it has become quite usual for politicians to insist on 'rigour' on behalf of parents, and students too, even when there is little evidence of concern among those groups. Teachers in the public sector are employed by tax-payers and it seems to me to be perfectly proper that we should accept, and agree with, a system which directly addresses the quality of teaching experienced by our students. We would want that for our own children, and therefore we should want it for other people's children too. This means that whatever the model of appraisal we go for, there should be within it or independent of it a mechanism for managing feedback to a teacher who is not providing the quality which students deserve, with steps to support change and ultimately to require change. This is never easy in teaching, where teachers often need support from colleagues, and loyalty to one's co-workers might be at the expense of the younger members of the school – the students.

One of the key requirements in any appraisal system will be the capacity occasionally to give and receive critical feedback, which many teachers seem to find difficult. It's worth treating as a specific training need, although perhaps not as the first priority. Certainly, agreeing a clear structure for giving and receiving all feedback about teaching is very helpful in the first instance, as 'scaffolding' which can be removed when the skills are strong enough to stand alone. More of this in the next chapter.

What 'Impact' do we want to achieve?

Before moving on, I want to return to the issue of 'impact' as a touchstone for the design of an appraisal process. I'm assuming that the core purpose of any appraisal model is to raise and sustain the quality of education offered to the school's students, and what distinguishes the three models I've described is the balance of 'pressure and support' to be used to achieve this. I'm also assuming that teachers will achieve most towards this end if they are 'engaged' with the task rather than just 'compliant'. The final assumption is about the potential capability of all teachers to improve their teaching if they wish to do so.

If these assumptions hold, and the desired impact is improved teaching going on every day, in the relative privacy of the classroom, then teachers need to be involved in decisions about what information is to be gathered, and how this will be done. If there's an observation checklist to be used in the classroom, teachers can design it. If there are questions to be asked of students, teachers can frame the questions. If a sample of parents or of students' work is to be chosen to gather information, then teachers can decide the nature of the sample. If there are pro-formas to be used, let the people who are going to use them design them. All this could be done as part of the whole-school 'training' which will be essential before the process starts, or gradually worked on later by a working group of staff, or volunteers. Someone will probably have been given the job of 'Co-ordinator' of the process, but that should not be interpreted to mean that he or she does it all alone, however much they want to and love sitting at home with the word-processor designing forms. The 'responsibility base' needs to be spread, more minds need to be involved, more people around who understand why and how decisions have been made, more investment in the outcome, more interest in how things work out. If teachers are learners, then the school is a big classroom, and we all achieve learning through engagement in relevant useful tasks rather than by the person in charge doing it all for us. It may take longer, and may not look as pretty or even be quite as good as it would have been under the control of one person, but it will probably achieve the same high quality by a slightly slower route.

Years ago I drew up a very simple diagram which reflected what I believed about the purpose of involving learners in the learning process. I still believe it, and have extended this to encompass teachers as learners too.

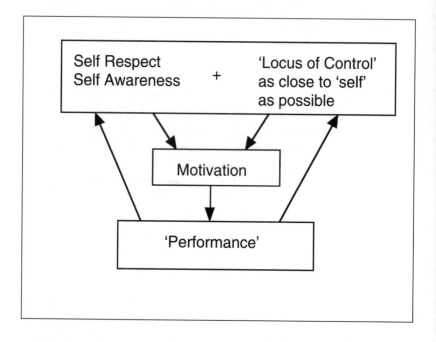

If the key to improved 'performance' (quantifiable 'results' as well as other important less quantifiable things) is motivation, not some pre-determined notion of ' innate capability', then we address motivation by building and sustaining self-respect; offering the learner useful feedback to improve self-awareness; and by giving the learner a clear sense of involvement in the learning circumstances which surround them. The concept of 'locus of control' is lifted straight out of research on motivation, and is powerfully reflected in the book on 'School Improvement – What Can Pupils Tell Us?' which I referred to earlier. Involvement can be encouraged in a wide range of ways: it does not mean handing over all control over learning to the learners. But without involvement, learning struggles to take root, encouraged only by deference to authority and fear of failure.

This connection of ideas, which underpins much of what I believe about teaching and assessment, was first applied only to younger learners, although it sprang from thinking about my own motivation. I've used it since to explore with teachers why their morale has been so adversely affected by their experience of the past decade and more, and what they can do to re-build it. Linking back to the New Right education agenda I sketched in the Preface, while teachers' self-respect was being systematically undermined by successive politicians, the curriculum was being re-designed by others – fast, and constantly re-drafted – pushing the 'locus of control' further and further out of the hands of the people who would have to make this new curriculum happen in the schools. After a while – about five years or so judging by our recent experience in the UK – teachers' sense of control over what they are being asked to do slowly begins to re-build, not by rejecting change but by 'customising' it, and this process happens much more successfully in some schools than in others, depending on the leadership skills (not just management skills) of the school's senior team.

Assessment plays a vital role in building and sustaining motivation and 'performance': the Learning School is one in which this purpose of assessment is systematically fostered, for students and teachers alike.

Key Points

1. Teachers are adult learners : much of what we know about effective learning applies to them too.

2. We need to identify whether the purpose of assessing teachers is for personal growth, contractual accountability, or school improvement.

3. 'Triangulation' involves gathering a range of evidence of teacher performance before reaching a judgement about it.

One big question

If we are sampling students' reactions or their work as evidence of effective teaching what should be the basis of the sample?

Chapter Five: Teacher Appraisal: Feedback and Feedforward

So far we've looked at the ways in which assessment information about teachers and teaching might be planned and gathered, applying the principles and questions explored in the first chapter. We ended up with 'Impact', but have left the 'So what?' question until now. Separate treatment of this question appears, on the basis of experience in England and Wales at least, to be necessary as this has been the weak link in the cycle.

During 1996 in England and Wales the Teacher Training Agency (TTA) and the Office for Standards in Education (OFSTED) conducted the second major evaluation of the national teacher appraisal scheme since it began in 1991. Their joint report acknowledged a change in the context since the start of the scheme: 'In many schools development planning is now seen as the mechanism for involving all those with a stake in the process in setting targets for improvement' was the comment on one aspect of this change. Many such schools, claimed the report, 'have already adapted their appraisal practices and produced a system for managing performance in which appraisal is a core element.' Interesting choice of words here.

The report recognised several positive outcomes of the appraisal process, including 'setting clear and practical targets' and 'the value of positive feedback and constructive critical comment', but noted also that 'these were not often seen in practice.' The list of weaknesses of much current appraisal practice was considerably longer than the list of strengths, and deserves to be seen in full – the emphasis of key phrases is as it appeared in the report.

'As well as highlighting the strengths of the current system, the review revealed key weaknesses which exist to a greater or lesser extent in many schools. These include:

a) **lack of rigour** in appraisal practice, eg. a failure to apply effectively the criteria for assessment, or to follow up weaknesses;

b) poor evaluation of the **impact** of appraisal on teaching quality and standards;

c) weakened the impact of appraisal on the quality of teachingthe failure to secure the role of the **line manager** as the appraiser, which has;

d) **component parts** of the process which are protracted, paper driven and bureaucratic and as such are time consuming and expensive;

e) **target setting for teachers,** which has often failed to focus sharply on improving teacher effectiveness in the classroom, and **for headteachers** which has failed to focus on school improvement;

f) **targets**, many of which were not specific, measurable, achievable or relevant;

g) infrequent **lesson observation** which is not as effective as other more reliable and valid forms of evidence which are now available. These forms include evidence from OFSTED inspections, internal evaluation including regular lesson observation and self-evaluation, and data from value-added work, external test results and teacher assessment;

h) the wide misinterpretation of the **confidentiality** of targets. This has led to a failure to ensure that appraisal is linked to school training and development, and has hampered plans for improvement in the quality of teaching and the performance of the school as a whole;

i) **the two year cycle** which has allowed the appraisal scheme to be perceived as extraneous to the normal cycle of management activity which focuses on school improvement;

j) the exclusion of the **chair of governors or a nominated governor** from the role of appraiser of the headteacher. This fails to recognise the local management responsibilities and accountabilities of governing bodies;

k) the **low priority** accorded to appraisal within many individual schools. In addition, according to many respondents to the review, appraisal has not been given sufficient priority and status in OFSTED inspections.

According to responses received, these weaknesses tend to occur in schools where the appraisal system has not developed significantly since its introduction in 1991, and are most apparent in schools which have failed to develop systems for improving teacher effectiveness.' (Taken from TTA/OFSTED: *Review of Headteacher and Teacher Appraisal - Summary of Evidence, 1997*).

I hope my readers in other countries will bear with this detailed analysis of the experience in England and Wales, where the 1991 legislation produced an approach to appraisal much like the 'personal growth' model identified in the previous chapter. If you check back with the characteristics of that model, you will see the relationship with the comments in the report. Clearly, the implication of the TTA and OFSTED's findings is that teacher appraisal should be linked much more closely than before to school development and improving teaching and learning.

My aim here, against this backdrop of experience, is to suggest ways in which the feedback and target-setting stages of the appraisal process can be managed to improve their impact, by applying the principles we have already looked at in Chapters One, Two and Three.

In Chapter Four we looked at how valid and reliable data might be gathered: now we move on to the 'So What?' question. In real terms, therefore, the teacher has already

- reflected on her teaching over the past few months, her achievement of targets she may have set previously, the difficulties she may be encountering and further improvements she wishes to make;

- decided what the focus for assessment of her teaching and other responsibilities should be in the appraisal process, hopefully seeing this as an opportunity to get some good feedback and to clarify her next steps;

- agreed with her appraiser the methods for gathering the necessary information, which has now been completed. This will probably usually have included observation of her teaching.

We pick up the story at this point: what happens next?

The Feedback Meeting

If this meeting is to be as useful as it needs to be, some preparation will be needed. Here are some things schools can do to improve the quality of this stage of the process.

1. As part of the initial training, address the question of what constitutes effective feedback, and develop a series of guidelines for giving feedback, like the simple list referred to in Chapter Two. Look back at the 'characteristics of

effective feedback'– page 43 – and then translate these items into some practical guidance about how best to offer feedback to a professional colleague.

2. These guidelines should also include some mention of how to receive feedback, not just in appraisal but in any professional context. Some of the suggestions I've seen related to this are:

- Listen to the feedback first rather than immediately rejecting or arguing with it.

- Be clear about what is being said, paraphrasing or repeating it if necessary, to help the other person clarify, and to make sure you have properly understood. You're asking for clarification, not change.

- Check out feedback with others, rather than relying on one source alone, and ask that others are honest with you.

- Ask for feedback that you want and don't get first time around. Help the appraiser to tell you what you want to know.

- Consider carefully what you will do as a result of the feedback.

There's nothing esoteric about this process. We use our intelligence, common sense and experience to arrive at these shared suggestions. Discussion of them before we write them down and agree to use them can be really helpful later in providing some structure for a potentially difficult process. Many people, of course, can manage perfectly well without such a structure, but others may find it useful, in the early stages at least.

3. Each of you reflects a little beforehand about the information as you see it. The 'appraiser' will probably make some notes about the key points she wants to include, and the 'appraisee' will have some questions she wants answers to, and some of her own perceptions and information which she wants to talk about.

4. Plan the time for the feedback conversation at your first meeting, to make sure that two busy people aren't having to set a time at too short notice. It is really important to have your conversation within a few days of classroom observation, for example, while the events are still fresh in the mind, and after you've a little while to reflect. That's not to say that nothing at all is said as the appraiser finishes their classroom observation: there's nothing worse than someone who has been in your classroom just getting up

and leaving the room. You will already have planned when you're going to meet, but basic politeness would expect a 'Thank you' at least, or a word or two, 'That was really helpful, thank you. I really liked the way you handled…', or 'Peter can be like that for me too, what are we going to do with him?'– something which recognises the teacher as a professional colleague and a co-worker in a challenging environment. The really detailed feedback you need to share will come later.

5. Make sure you have enough time planned for a proper conversation, including discussing targets, and recording your conclusions. You shouldn't be interrupted except in an emergency, and you will probably also want to be reasonably private. The number of minutes you'll need will vary, but it probably won't be less than 30 or more than 50. In the literature about creating the right conditions for such an interview / conversation you'll find all sorts of things about how to arrange the furniture, making eye-contact, and so on. The golden rule is that both the people involved should feel comfortable. What one person may take for granted may not suit another, so check your assumptions, remember this is a professional conversation not a power exercise or a therapy session, and take it from there.

6. Don't make too much of a meal out of writing the record of your discussion and its conclusions. These do not need to be models of deathless prose, just a functional and accurate record of the key points. I don't think the 'unstructured prose' method of record-keeping is useful here : something much simpler is perfectly OK.

One school I worked with had successfully implemented much of their appraisal system, but had got really stuck on the writing of 'appraisal statements'. These were to be a record of the appraisal findings and future targets for the teacher. Feedback was offered and targets discussed, and then the appraiser would go away to write the statement, checking the first draft with the teacher to ensure accurate recall of what had been agreed at their meeting. These statements were taking far too long to produce and in some cases just did not re-emerge. Targets were remembered partially or not at all, and the whole credibility of the exercise was in jeopardy because there appeared to be little formal output of an expensive process in terms of teacher time.

My suggestion was that they set aside 5-10 minutes at the end of the feedback and target setting event to record then and there the agreed key points, in a simple pro-forma, signed by both parties . The design of the pro-forma which the school developed and used was this.

Date	Agreed focus area(s)	Key points of feedback	Next steps (NB 'SMART' Targets)
Signed _____ Date _____			

With this preparation, feedback can have a much more 'businesslike' feel: Both parties know what they're trying to achieve, the conditions are conducive, agreed guidelines can be recalled and used to structure the conversation, and there's a relevant and visible outcome in the completed and signed proforma.

Offering and Receiving Critical Feedback

In the great majority of cases, feedback about a colleague's teaching and other responsibilities will, given intelligent preparation and useful information , be one of the most helpful professional events we can provide. Far from being a burden or a worry, many teachers have welcomed the opportunity for the specific recognition of their skills and qualities, and regard such feedback as part of their professional entitlement. For others however, the process has brought anxiety, not just about feedback they might receive, but about the task of **providing** critical feedback, telling a colleague something they may not want to hear.

All the suggestions we've made so far, about agreed procedures, preparation and so on, will help, but at the end of the day critical feedback will sometimes have to be offered, and attended to, and improvements made. We have to see this through, not just because that's what the government or the school system or someone else requires of us but because the first concern of all schools is the students. All schools aspire to offer their students the best possible opportunity for successful learning: this is where the rubber hits the road.

Recognising a duty to our students as the prime reason for ensuring clear critical feedback where it is warranted, let's step back from the specific circumstances of school life for a moment and see what advice is available on the skills of giving critical feedback. The Counselling and Career Development Unit , based in Leeds, have a well-deserved reputation for providing excellent guidance on effective communication in all sorts of organisations, including schools. They have a special leaflet on the 'The Skills of Giving Negative Feedback'. Listing the concerns that all of us have about giving such feedback – 'Will they get upset? Will it affect the relationship? Will it make any difference?' and so on - a further question is added – 'Can we afford not to give the feedback: what will be the consequences of doing nothing?'

Suggestions are offered about how to maximise the effect and minimise the pain of critical feedback, keeping it on a thoroughly professional level, but not avoiding the key issues. The feedback is the start of the next stage of development, not the end of the final stage, so it helps to check that what has been said is properly understood. Asking the person to paraphrase what we've said to them, and to comment about it will help to clarify and begin the search for productive next steps. When the feedback has to be critical, here's some specific advice:

- Try to preface negative feedback with something positive, and specific.

- Be as specific as possible, pinpointing behaviours that can and need to be changed.

- Always check to see that they have heard you correctly.

- Ask them whether they agree or not.

- Ask them if they have ever heard anything similar about themselves before.

- Ask them if they can think of anything they could do differently.

- Ask them to specify what they are going to do differently, from when, and how they will find out if it has been effective.

- Ask them to think or talk through the consequences of acting or not acting on the feedback given.

You'll notice that the person receiving the feedback is very much involved here in reacting to and planning from the specific feedback he or she has received. The aim of the exercise is to improve the person's performance, in specific ways, pretty quickly, and to check that it really happens. It's honest and rigorous and clear.

I have had some interesting reactions to these ideas from people who seem to think that the only thing to do with teachers experiencing difficulties is to frighten or shame them into improvement. Perhaps they have similar ideas about how to get the best out of students too. Getting angry, raising your voice, or dominating the conversation may reassert what you feel is your professional control over the teacher; it may relieve your own frustration on behalf of the students; it might even have an impact in the short term as the teacher is constantly watched and monitored; but will it cause a continued improvement, when the monitoring has relaxed and things appear to be back to normal?

Sometimes, perhaps, when feedback is offered in very punitive ways, the issue has gone beyond the hope or expectation of improvement, and has become a disciplinary matter, in which case quite a different approach may be needed. In a professional environment, all these situations need to be approached in a considered way. All schools and school systems have policies for ensuring minimum levels of professional competence, and steps to be taken if this minimum is not forthcoming. These procedures are carefully framed, quite rightly, to protect a teacher from unfair treatment, and will also have to be used to protect students from the unfairness of their learning being adversely affected by very poor teaching.

Taking care to balance the needs and rights of all the parties involved, schools will need to establish clear and just procedures to monitor the teaching of teachers in difficulties. The question is whether the appraisal process should be used as the first step in such a process. This is a tricky one. No one wants procedures which are more elaborate and bureaucratic than is absolutely necessary. Evidence of a teacher's performance will be needed in any enquiry regarding their 'competence', but seeking such evidence through the appraisal process and then using it for disciplinary purposes threatens to undermine the purpose and honesty required in successful appraisal for the sake of the more speedy pursuit of the relatively small number of incompetent teachers in our schools. There are many more teachers whose teaching can be improved than there are teachers whose teaching needs to be stopped.

My own view, with which others might disagree, is that the gathering of information for competence proceedings should be a separate exercise, quite disconnected from information gathering for the regular and systematic appraisal of all teaching staff. This may occasionally lead to duplication of effort, but this is a price worth paying if it enables most teachers to be honest about the difficulties they experience and want to put right, without fear that such honesty may lead them into a competence procedure. Evidence for competence proceedings will be gathered over a longer time, and in a greater variety of contexts than is manageable or necessary for appraisal. Just as high-stake student assessment puts greater emphasis on reliability, so it does also for high-stake assessment of teachers. One of the potential problems of the contractual accountability model of teacher assessment is that it

is high stake for everyone, all the time, and the information gathering process can become very problematic as safeguards are built in to protect both employers and employees.

This separation of appraisal from competence is not about avoiding hard decisions: hard decisions will and must continue to be made when teaching is simply not good enough. But, when two purposes are potentially involved in any assessment process, if we try to combine them for ease of manageability we run the risk of sacrificing one purpose to the other. The purpose of assessment for improvement is too crucial to put at risk.

SMART Target-setting for Teachers

Maybe it's because the quality of feedback to teachers has not always been high that the quality of target-setting has also been so patchy within and among our schools. As we saw earlier, feedback and feedforward are very closely connected. Being clear and specific about next steps is extraordinarily difficult if we lack clear and specific information about our current learning strengths and needs. Improve the feedback and good target-setting will follow. Target-setting is a learned skill, up to a point, beyond which it is an attitude of mind. It assumes positive potential and a belief in the future: cynics make terrible target-setters because they have neither. Target-setting also assumes that we are confident enough to stretch and risk occasional failure without fear of blame, recrimination or ridicule. Some learning atmospheres are supportive of these feelings: others are quite certainly not.

> *This experience is not typical, but was a powerful reminder to me of how important the staffroom atmosphere can be for teachers as learners. I was in a school which was, to its credit, trying to address the growing achievement gap between boys and girls which was clearly indicated in their GCSE results at 16+. In terms of 'passing grades' in five or more subjects, the girls were doing exactly twice as well*

as the boys, in the same school, with the same teachers, the same exams, the same community, and the same year. We worked together during the day on possible strategies to encourage more commitment and more effective learning among the boys.

As the teachers discussed ideas, asked questions of me and each other, and made suggestions, it became clear that a small group of the men on the staff made a regular habit of what you could call 'teasing' each other and anyone else who appeared to be interested in research, or used academic terms, or made strong suggestions which would involve real change, or different ways of working. It was banter rather than rudeness and one of this group told me that this humour made the school a great place to work. Other members of staff, male and female, told me more privately that this was typical of the atmosphere in the staffroom. Jokes flew, usually at the expense of others. For some it felt unsafe to speak up or to be seen to be trying hard, for fear of the ridicule which would probably result. More than a few were really fed up with it, but didn't want to be accused of being 'party poopers' or spoilsports, or just boring.

An outsider has a great advantage in this situation: he or she can speak the unspeakable, draw the flack if there is any, and give others the chance to use the opportunity if they choose to do so. So I did. Towards the end of the day, in as good-natured and direct a way as I could, I suggested to the whole staff that teachers are learners too, who also need a reasonably safe atmosphere in which they will be taken seriously, allowed to make an overt effort, and allowed to ask questions even if others know the answers. If they were prepared to use humour to intimidate each other, then maybe something similar could be inhibiting the boys, whose awareness of each other was a stronger influence on them than anything else.

*Did it make any difference? Maybe not, but I tried, and
hopefully the issue would be aired again. Learning schools
need staffrooms as well as classrooms with atmospheres
conducive to learning.*

SMART target-setting is as important for teachers as it is for their
students, and forms a central feature of effective appraisal.
Whenever I'm working with teachers on these issues I remind
them of the acronym – Specific, Measurable, Achievable, Relevant,
Time-Related – and go through each part with them, just as I did
in Chapter Three. When at the end of our work I ask them to set
themselves some targets, I structure it quite carefully. The first
request is that they review their notes or thoughts from the
sessions or the handouts we've looked at, just to bring back to
mind the ideas and implications which will have been in their
minds as we've worked. Then I give them just a few minutes to
write down three targets for themselves for the coming term or
semester, or some other reasonable medium-term time frame.
Next they work with a partner for between five and ten minutes,
and each of them acts as 'critical friend' for the other, using
SMART as the prompt for questions about the appropriacy,
specificity, and so on of the targets which have been written
down. It's an 'interrogation' in the nicest possible sense; it's
mutual, it's very focused and it's quick. When they have finished,
I ask them to go back to their own original targets and rewrite
them, making use of the feedback and further thought which it
has prompted. Almost every time, with just a few minutes
reflection and feedback, the second draft of their targets is an
improvement on the first draft.

Does it matter what we write down when it's all in our heads
anyway? Yes I think it does. Even a day or two after we've written
something down we may look at it again and see only what was
written, not the wealth of thought behind it. If there's nothing
written, our memories may file it away but then lose the file.
Memory is too crowded and too fickle – at least mine is – to be
trusted with information which should have a bearing on our

actions for months to come. Targets need to be recorded as clearly and explicitly as we can, as SMART as we can manage, and kept somewhere as a regular reminder. They were written to guide our actions and that's what they should do, not just for the week after the review and the week before the next one, but all the weeks in between.

Identifying Staff Development Needs

A further outcome of the appraisal process, apart from the individual's own targets, is usually the identification of staff development needs, which will then be addressed through the school's staff development activities. For some schools this has created a headache for the Staff Development Coordinator : the appraisal process generates an unpredictable quantity and potential cost of staff development needs, which must somehow be met with a finite and limited amount of staff development money. To make matters more difficult, some staff have difficulty distinguishing between staff development and in-service training, and assume that all in-service training has to be provided off-site, preferably somewhere with a fancy lunch. This is not to say that teachers as professional people do not deserve high quality support such as is apparently available to other professions. But the only real measure of quality is what impact the experience has on the need it was designed to meet, regardless of what kind of experience this might be, or where it takes place, or whether or not you get a choice of desserts.

In the first round of appraisal in some schools development needs were identified and money allocated as it went along, with the result that all the year's money had been allocated before all the needs had been identified. Schools tried to forestall this by agreeing beforehand the amount of staff development money to be available to each member of staff, but such ostensible equity took no account of the diversity of need. Why is life so complicated? Formulas can be developed to balance these conflicting pressures, but many schools have had to become far more creative than before about providing opportunities for professional learning, without spending beyond the limits of the staff development budget.

When targets are more specific, the task of providing the necessary support becomes easier in some respects. Some of the specific elements could be provided in school, or in the community, or through links with another school. Role-shadowing can be really useful, or classroom observation for a specific purpose, or an in-school action research project, properly organised and accredited through a partnership with higher education.

However plans for learning support for teachers are made, they must be closely related to the original targets, and 'sustainable'. The targets themselves will need to be reviewed periodically, to keep them fresh. This should not necessitate a formal interview: an informal check —5 minutes, 'How's it going?'—will probably suffice to prevent them being neglected for long periods, resurrected only when the next annual review is imminent, by which time it's too late to address them properly. The question of who checks will of course vary from one model of appraisal to another: in the personal growth model it will be the chosen appraisal partner; in the contractual accountability model it will be the line manager; in the school improvement model it will be someone from your team, or the team leader. The more open and shared the targets are, the more likely it is that they will remain fresh. In the school improvement model, ten minutes of an occasional team meeting could be devoted to checking and discussing how people are getting on towards achieving their agreed targets.

In the next chapter, I try to knit together the various strands which support sound assessment and effective learning, and envisage a school where all the learners, adult and child, individually and collectively, are basing their learning on these principles. When students, teachers, and the school as a whole are all simultaneously engaged with planning, organising, evaluating and looking forward, the effect is more than the sum of its parts. What develops is what we can call the 'Learning School'.

Key Points

1. Schools find it useful to have agreed guidelines about the best ways to give and receive professional feedback.

2. Not giving critical feedback where necessary can create more problems than doing so.

3. Staff development involves a wide range of activities, and needs to be closely linked with different teachers' needs and with the school's agreed goals.

One big question

Is it really fair to allocate the same annual amount of staff development money to every member of staff? What other 'formula' would you use, if any?

Chapter Six:
Towards The Learning School

Here are three 'cycles', each representing part of every school's activity.

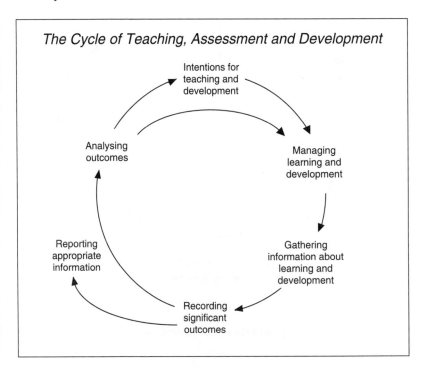

The Cycle of Teaching, Assessment and Development

Intentions for teaching and development

Managing learning and development

Gathering information about learning and development

Recording significant outcomes

Reporting appropriate information

Analysing outcomes

In this one, the learning of individual students or groups of students is our object – for which we plan, manage activities, gather, record and report information about outcomes, and use the information to plan further. The component parts of the cycle are closely linked to each other and the process is only complete when it 'feeds forward' into next steps to improve learning. This cycle was the starting point for my book on 'Assessment for Learning'.

131

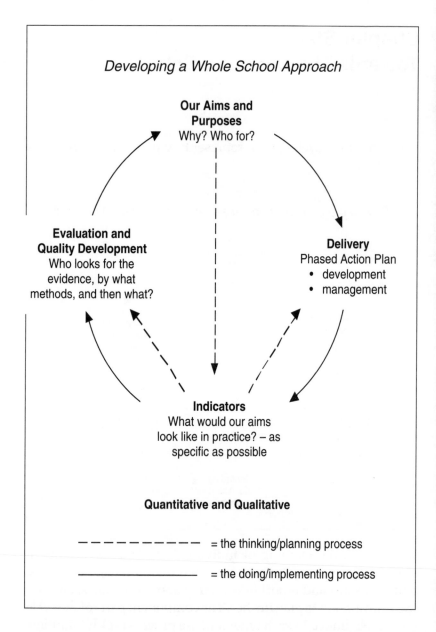

Developing a Whole School Approach

Our Aims and Purposes
Why? Who for?

Evaluation and Quality Development
Who looks for the evidence, by what methods, and then what?

Delivery
Phased Action Plan
- development
- management

Indicators
What would our aims look like in practice? – as specific as possible

Quantitative and Qualitative

– – – – – – – – – = the thinking/planning process

———————— = the doing/implementing process

This diagram is about building effective monitoring and evaluation into school development planning – in other words assessing the school – and I wrote about it in 'School Self Review'.

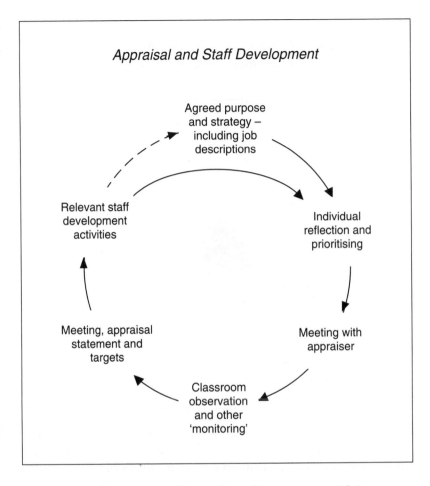

In this cycle, the learner is the teacher who pursues, with 'pressure and support' from others, the information, feedback, targets and learning activities he will need to meet and go beyond required standards of teaching competence.

In many schools these three spirals of development are being pursued simultaneously but separately: the connections between them may be implicit, or not considered at all. In the Learning School. the three are clearly and explicitly connected. In fact they overlap. School Evaluation, Teacher Appraisal and Student Assessment.

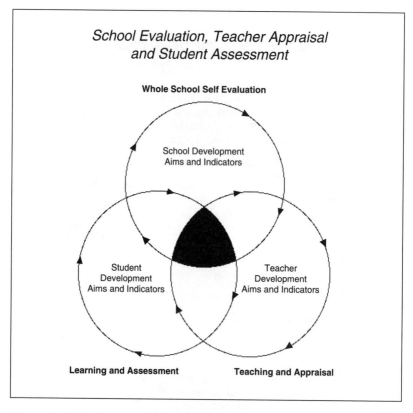

School Evaluation, Teacher Appraisal and Student Assessment

Whole School Self Evaluation

School Development Aims and Indicators

Student Development Aims and Indicators

Teacher Development Aims and Indicators

Learning and Assessment   **Teaching and Appraisal**

The overlap between them is partly about underpinning principles, and partly about focus. The underpinning principles are the ones we have examined earlier in this book:

- the importance of gathering information about outcomes which balances the requirements of validity, reliability, manageability, cost and public/political acceptability;

- the need for specific, timely, useful feedback;

- the need for both 'skill and will' to set and check targets. **The shared focus, the place where the cycles overlap, is the classroom, where both teaching and learning happen and where school improvement plans become reality. There is no more important place for all of us to focus our attention.**

Treating these three development cycles as overlapping parts of the same enterprise has the added bonus of helping the school to become more efficient as well as more effective. Potentially time-consuming procedures can be merged. Examples?

- Staff development about feedback and feedforward for teachers can be used to enhance teachers' skills in giving feedback to their students and helping students to set effective targets for themselves.

- Classroom monitoring – of students' learning as well as teachers' teaching – by team leaders, Heads of Department or Co-ordinators can be combined with developing useful feedback and improvement targets for individual teachers.

The 'personal growth' model of teacher appraisal was being discussed, without great enthusiasm, by the science team in a high school. They talked to each other about the particular feedback each of them had sought in the private appraisal process they had experienced, and realised the commonalities and differences among the areas they had selected. They then moved on to the more formal purpose of their meeting, which was to agree their Science Team targets for the coming year, as part of the whole school development plan. As they got started, someone interrupted. 'Hang on a minute', he said, 'go back to what we were talking about before. We each have three focus areas for our appraisal next year, right? Why don't we each 'donate' one of those three to the team, and choose a target from our team development plan. If we as a team want to focus next year on giving more challenge to more able students in the Lower School, then why don't all of us who teach in the Lower School choose that as a focus? Then we work on it together as well as separately, compare notes, share ideas, learn from each other, divide the monitoring between us. It would be more fun and more useful than beavering away on our own. We could pick a different shared focus for people who won't teach in the Lower School next year. We could even share findings with each other, as the year goes along— it would just mean using one of our regular meetings for that rather than using all of those meetings for day-to-day business.'

Everyone in the team agreed to give it a try.

At the next Heads of Department meeting, the Head of Science explained what they were going to do: 'Hope nobody minds,' he said, 'we know this is not quite what the appraisal procedures said we had to do, but we just thought it would be a good idea.' The Deputy Head who was chairing the meeting checked around. The Head of Art said they might be interested too because they worked so closely together that it made sense. The Technology rep. said that her team had talked vaguely about such an idea, and they too had made challenging the more able students one of their team targets. Could they meet to share ideas with the Science team?

You can see the next step coming I'm sure. With encouragement from the Deputy Head, the meeting agreed to pick up one target from the school development plan for the coming year, and to suggest to all their teams that this should be one of the three focus areas for every member of staff. It would then be supported by one of the school's staff development days early in the new year. Monitoring of the target could draw on a wealth of evidence, gathered across the whole school. Science and Technology agreed, without prompting, to monitor each other, to bring in a different way of doing things, and to ask more searching questions about methods and outcomes.

What about those teachers who chose not to be part of this more collective exercise? While it was being tried out in the coming school year they had every right to continue with a more private process. A whole school decision about

*future years' procedures was left until they could see what
the potential and the pitfalls might be.*

*I was not personally party to this: it was recounted to me
as a story about the failings of the personal growth model,
and is a clear example of how 'appraisal for school
improvement' can grow naturally given the right
conditions.*

*What do you think the potential and the pitfalls might be
for such developments in your school, if they don't already
happen?*

As part of my work over the past fifteen years or so I have worked
with hundreds of whole school staffs. I have not set out deliberately
to study them as groups, or to analyse the way they work
together, their shared assumptions, or their relative effectiveness.
Because I see them away from the students, and sometimes away
from their normal working environment, my impressions must
remain impressions, but they accumulate over the years to the
point where I begin to recognise some of the characteristics of
schools which are 'Learning Schools'.

The school in the story just above did not decide to become a
'Learning School' but it was well on the way to being one. You
could say this was just accidental, but was it? Certain procedures
were in place which provided fertile ground for the seeds to
grow: subject teams were encouraged to contribute to the school
development plan; individual teams met regularly and the
atmosphere in some of those meetings at least was open enough
for ideas to be generated and followed through; the Heads of
Departments meetings were chaired by someone sensible enough
to let something happen which was not on the planned agenda
but in which she recognised the potential; the school didn't rush
to change its procedures but let people come on board when they
felt ready to do so.

The Conditions of Learning

In their books 'School Improvement: What Can Pupils Tell Us?', Jean Ruddock and her co-authors review in the final chapter their conclusions about conditions which positively affect young people's learning, using evidence drawn from extensive interviews with them.

Six principles are presented which confirm much of the previous research about school improvement: respect; fairness; autonomy; intellectual challenge; social support; security. In addition, the authors highlight the importance of organisational structures such as student grouping, and rewards and sanctions; relationships with teachers, enabling all students to feel that they can achieve something worthwhile, for example; and listening to the voice of the students themselves, who have useful and important insight to offer about how the school has helped them to learn and develop, or not.

Suggestions are made about the pursuit of all these principles and areas for development, and the authors are aware that these may sound like 'rather vague and virtuous exhortations'. I have similar reservations about the suggestions that follow about generating effective conditions for the learning of teachers as well as students, the more so because I have not painstakingly interviewed the teachers with whom I work, but just watched and listened to them over a long period of time. It may well be that I have heard and seen that which resonates with me as a learner myself, and these conclusions should be treated as personal, but I'll offer them anyway. I'll describe first the characteristics of the Learning School which affect the teachers as well as the students, and then suggest some steps that schools could take towards this goal.

Some Characteristics of the Learning School

- Relationships matter as well as procedures and systems.

- People communicate with each other quite openly and directly, and with respect.

- There's a balance between planned directions and the flexibility to respond to unanticipated events.

- Developments are discussed not in terms of 'them' and 'us', or blame when things don't work as expected, but as ways of thinking about what to do better next time.

- There's an expectation that people are both willing and able to try new ways of working: an assumption of potential for improvement.

- The adult learners as well as the younger students are 'engaged' with their learning rather than merely 'compliant' with organisational or other requirements.

- There's a climate of curiosity which translates into action not just endless discussion. People who want to try things are not discouraged or undermined by others.

I could add more characteristics of 'Learning Schools' and so could you, drawing on our experience and intelligence we need to turn experience into learning. Many of us have experienced learning **teams**, but learning **schools** are not so common. Some smaller schools have the great advantage of sheer physical proximity, but sometimes when relationships are troublesome this can inhibit rather than encourage the climate we need. Sometimes, too, sheer complacency can undermine the energy and curiosity the learning school needs. If we feel we have no need to learn, then why bother – we can just coast along. At the other extreme, day-to-day survival in difficult circumstances can undermine the chance to learn, even if the will and skill are both there. So much energy is invested in just coping that there's not enough left over to learn.

However the details of this picture develop, the exercise can be frustrating. This is a school where you would love to work, and the comparison between that and where you work now can sometimes begin to gnaw away at you.

> *We've all had frustrations in our work and careers. Once, some years ago now, I shared mine with someone whose judgement I respected. He listened patiently and then offered what I thought at the time was pretty brutal advice. 'You've got three choices,' he said, 'Change the system, change yourself, or get out.' The first option I had tried and failed, the second I was too pig-headed to contemplate. I took the third option and don't regret it.*

Rather than add to these frustrations by adding more and more features to the goal of the Learning School, thereby making it seem more and more unattainable, I'm proposing instead to make some suggestions about making progress towards this goal. This does not and cannot constitute a recipe to be followed: the ingredients may have some commonality from one school to another, but the way you mix them, the oven temperature and the cooking time will vary in line with the uniqueness of every school. I've gathered the ingredients onto three plates—staff development; procedures and systems; and ways of thinking. All the suggestions are drawn from schools I've encountered, so you and your school may well recognise things you already do.

Steps Towards the Learning School

Staff Development

- Start by finding out as much as possible about the skills, experience, talents, learning styles and abilities of all the teachers, and the other adults who work in the school, in whatever capacity.

- Identify what each of the learners is able and willing to offer to the school's development, and wherever possible create opportunities for this contribution to be made.

- Identify the areas which each of the adults would most like to develop further, and wherever possible create opportunities for this development. There needs to be a 'continuing professional development' plan for each of the school's adult learners, coordinated and managed by a senior member of staff.

- Both of these carry costs in both money and time. So, shine a very strong light on all the school's existing procedures which involve the teachers working separately from the students – meetings and staff development days for example – and analyse as carefully as possible where the existing staff development money is spent. Is all this time and money clearly connected to the school's stated aims and to the development targets it has set itself? Could these connections be strengthened by a shift of emphasis, by a change in the organisation and management of some meetings, for example?

- Where teachers do go out of school to pursue a particular development, plan how to make the most effective use of what they have experienced and learned. This could be done through a 'poster' in the staff room, or a written report (preferably with an agreed format, to make it easier to complete and to read), or a brief presentation to the most relevant group of colleagues if not to the whole staff. At the very least, always take an interest in what someone has learned and what they might do next as a result.

- Keep a small reserve of money or time available for which people can bid if they have a particular project or line of enquiry they wish to pursue, and use any external funding you can find for such a purpose. Somewhere within the school or the governing body will be someone with good 'resource investigator' skills: their task can be to research all external staff development funding possibilities.

- In smaller schools, where the quantity and flexibility of available time and funds is less, and the 'gene pool' of skills and interests is smaller, team up with other local schools to share ideas and work together. Make use of any available technology to put people in touch with each other and with the wider world, and avoid the feeling of professional isolation which can stultify learning.

- Be prepared to pursue external accreditation of teachers' learning wherever possible. Forthcoming proposals about Continuing Professional Development from the Teacher Training Agency in England and Wales should help to establish a structure for the formal provision and recognition of CPD, and one wonders why this wasn't begun many years ago. Teaching is one of the few professions, in this country at least, where someone can be qualified to teach through a 30 week post-graduate programme and then continue to do so for the remainder of what could be a 30 year career without any requirement to refresh and develop his or her skills. Of course many teachers and schools already take professional development seriously, but teachers have no current requirement to take the opportunities available to them. We rely on teachers' personal and largely intrinsic motivation to learn, and in some cases this will not be sufficient. Even when intrinsic goals—job satisfaction rather than financial reward—are the prime motive, learning deserves to be formally recognised through further qualification and certification, without necessarily going for a further degree.

A Portfolio of Achievement for Teachers

Portfolios have been in use with younger learners for a decade and more, as part of the process of Recording Achievement in the UK, and as a major feature of 'alternative' assessment systems in North America. Portfolios for learners are usually developed to exemplify and illuminate the learner's progress and achievements; they can be used as both a support for and an outcome of periodic discussions with a 'reviewer' or 'mentor'; they can be part of the learner's self presentation to a parent, or a future employer, or the 'gatekeeper' to the next stage in their education. (Various purposes and styles of portfolios are discussed in Chapter 5 of 'Assessment for Learning').

Learners' portfolios will contain certificated evidence of learning – exam certificates, for example – alongside selected samples of work done, exemplifying learning strengths and difficulties overcome. Such items may jostle in the carefully organised folder with photos, or newspaper cuttings, or video clips, or letters from people connected with the students' learning. Every item will be 'annotated' to explain its origin, and the reasons for its selection, and arranged into sections, so that readers can find their way through it. Students will have spent time not only discussing what to include, but how to present the completed portfolio to others, recognising the specific elements a particular 'audience' might be interested in.

> *One of the Colleges of Education in New Zealand has developed portfolios for the assessment of post-graduate teacher training. Before their placement in schools students discuss the specific objectives and expected outcomes of the placement. They are given the responsibility of selecting, annotating and presenting evidence of their achievement of the stated outcomes, and this portfolio plays a central part of the assessment of 'the practicum'.*

> *In another New Zealand College of Education, 3-year degree students are required to gather evidence of their achievements and progress into a portfolio which is reviewed two or three times a year with a 'mentor', with targets for the following months resulting from this discussion. This forms the basis of evidence gathering by the student, and the starting point of the next review.*

Students in school do it; student teachers do it; if teachers are learners, then how long will it take before such a staff development structure becomes commonplace in our schools? A portfolio of achievement for teachers could serve the same formative and summative purposes as it does for other learners, built into the procedures for appraisal and continuing professional development. As happens elsewhere, portfolios can add colour and life and a sense of reality to the assessment and target-setting process. They provoke more interesting conversations and appeal to a wider range of thinking and learning styles. Of course there would need to be some attention given to the minimum requirements of a portfolio for teachers, just as there needs to be attention to the pursuit of minimum professional competency, but beyond that the learners can flourish, because they want to not just because they have to.

Structures and systems in the Learning School

- Involve each teacher in drawing up a clear outline of his or her roles and responsibilities. This 'job description' is not a list of tasks : how the responsibilities are fulfilled should be thought through by the person – 'engagement not just compliance' – with whatever careful monitoring is needed to ensure that key areas are properly covered. The type and degree of monitoring should also be 'customised', differentiated to fit need and circumstances like all good delegation.

- Broaden the number of people given a real opportunity to contribute to school policy developments to maximise the talent the school can draw upon and to give those who want it the chance to grow, to build on their   ths and overcome weaker areas in the real lif   text of the school. This may mean that your teachers learn faster, and more effectively, and consequently move on, but they will add to the energy of the school before they do, and provide encouragement to others. This may also mean opening up some parts of a job for which someone had previously been paid, but which may not have been done as effectively as possible. Loosening or re-arranging roles and responsibilities may be necessary to allow in some fresh ideas: win-win solutions to the question of who gets what jobs within the school cannot always be found, but sometimes they can if we are prepared to think more creatively.

- In structural terms, look again at the formal groupings within the school, especially in larger schools where the layers of hierarchy can sometimes suffocate the energy and curiosity the Learning School needs. Where staff size permits, the creation of school-wide task groups with clear aims, resource parameters, time frames and responsibilities can be extremely effective in harnessing the potential collective talent of the staff, but only so long as the senior policy makers are prepared to take their proposals seriously, and act upon them whenever possible.

- To allow the flexibility to respond to some unanticipated outcomes and ideas, don't make any school or teaching plans so tight that no response is possible. Of course school plans need a clear sense of direction, but that should not necessarily mean that the focus of every staff development day is planned a year or more ahead, that every meeting agenda is timed and fixed, that every last drop of money is specifically committed beforehand.

- Whole-school formats for planning and information gathering do add a useful sense of coherence to the activities of individuals and groups, but there needs to be some empty space in them too, or we run the risk of squeezing out the spontaneity, creativity, fun, idiosyncrasy, which make Learning Schools exciting places to work. You're never quite sure what might happen next. If the senior management want to be absolutely in control, all the time, that will have an impact on the school identical to the attempt to impose absolute teacher control on the classroom, and teachers can be a lot more subversive than students.

- Take monitoring and evaluation seriously and plan them into the school's systems and structures, to keep the feedback and feedforward loops working effectively. This may mean doing some quite specific staff development in these areas, as many of us have had very little opportunity to learn the skills and techniques we need in the normal progression of our careers.

Ways of thinking

- Avoid the 'image-fixing' which researchers have found so prevalent among teachers about their students, and which learners find so difficult to shake off. Teachers and senior managers in schools often have 'fixed images' of each other as well as their students. So-and-so is 'no good' at something, or 'can't be trusted', or 'will never make a good teacher'.

An extreme, but real, example. A successful and talented Headteacher of my acquaintance had been 'labelled' early in her career by her Headteacher, who had written in her file that she was a 'good classroom teacher but should never be allowed anywhere near management responsibilites'. Fortunately this note was discovered by the new incoming Headteacher, who checked it out, discovered it to be based on one incident in the teacher's first year, six years previously, and tore it up.

- As teachers, we are often challenged to assert a belief in the potential capability – of some kind, not necessarily academic – of every one of our students. Theories of 'multiple intelligence' have required us to recognise the limitations of much of what is offered in schools, and to accept how many students dismissed by schools go on to have successful lives out there in the world. As teachers and school managers do we have the same belief in the capability of all our colleagues? Do we identify and respect their 'multiple intelligences'? Do we have the time and resources to draw the best possible teaching and development out of every single adult learner in the school? I suspect the answer is 'No', but that should not prevent us from trying really hard to do all these things.

Inevitably, and in exceptional cases, the needs of the younger learners do take precedence in the end. At some point, after all the care and support and pressure we can offer to some teachers, their achievement is just not as good as their students need and deserve, and the students' needs come first. Finding the balance between the needs of different groups of learners, or between the individual learner and his/her peers, has always been a dilemma: regarding teachers as learners just adds another layer to those hard decisions.

Motivation

At the heart of any learning, whatever the age of the learner, is the issue of motivation. All educators recognise the impact of motivation on learning, although we may disagree about the source of motivation and how it can be developed and sustained. The young people in the study by Ruddock et al have some very revealing things to say about it, but generalisations are very difficult to establish. My own thoughts on the matter are no doubt as personal as anyone else's, although I have read and listened and pondered a great deal, first of all about the motivation of school students, then about the motivation of teachers—who are now my main clients – and of course about my own motivation.

After much deliberation and soul-searching, the major piece of the picture fell into place for me ten years ago, at a conference in Seattle, listening to an academic from Hawaii talking about motivation among adolescents. (Place-dropping is one of my big problems - please forgive me.) He talked at length about the notion of 'locus of control' which of course I should have come across before, but I hadn't. Low motivation, he explained, stemmed from a feeling that one's life is determined by forces quite beyond one's control. Things just happen, arbitrarily. Sometimes they may be good things, sometimes bad, but you just wait passively for them. If you have absolute faith that this arbitrary power is actually benevolent and protective - through belief in a benign God for example - you might be comforted enough to hang in there, but there's nothing you can do to affect your fate.

Within the limited context of a person's learning life, at school for instance, what can the notion of 'locus of control' tell us about the attitudes and structures which may provide successful 'conditions for learning?

Before pursuing this notion further, to connect it to the basic premises of this book, let me explore the other pre-requisites which seem to me at least to underpin motivation in the Learning School, for all the learners, young and not so young. Self-respect as part of motivation – unless you believe that fear of shame and blame is what inspires effective learning, in which case you probably stopped reading several chapters ago. Perhaps more accurately we should use the term 'self-efficacy' which is concerned with individuals' belief in their competence to accomplish specific tasks : self-respect in relation to what we do and what is specifically expected of us, rather than in relation to who we are. There is a high correlation in studies of young learners' motivation between self-efficacy and the ability to persevere when difficulties are encountered. I wonder if this same connection also affects teachers as adult learners.

Self-efficacy is very closely connected to self-awareness in learning. How do we find out what we are potentially capable of, or the strengths and weaknesses our current performance displays? Without accurate and specific feedback about our learning, and good information about the requirements of the next learning task, can I be really motivated and given a real chance to learn effectively? This is where it gets personal: if I have no real idea what I'm being asked to do, and where the gap is between that and what I'm doing now, I suspect I'm being set up to fail, and I get cross.

It may be that this element of my motivation is part of my urge for at least some control over my learning life. In fact, this urge for me may be greater than is comfortable. Anyone who is both happily single and self-employed must have a strong need for control over their own life. My pathology aside however, self-efficacy, good feedback about learning, and a 'locus of control' which allows the learner to feel involved in their own learning, if not in control of it make up the basic ingredients of effective motivation.

The distinction between intrinsic and extrinsic goals is not a major issue here. What matters is the opportunity to understand what are the external standards against which your learning is to be judged. I believe this is one reason why so many assessment theorists and writers, and others too, conclude that competitive and norm-referenced assessment procedures should be avoided until the final high-stake selective assessments require some attention in the final years of high school. Norm-referencing, in which results are determined in relation to the performance of others, removes some of the feeling of control over your own performance. 'What do I need to do to get an 'A' ?' 'Do better than a certain percentage of your peers.' To quote again from Terry Crookes' 1988 research review:

> *'It is hard to see any justification before the final year or so of high school for placing much emphasis on using classroom evaluation for normative grading of student achievement, given the evidence that normative grading (with the social comparison and inter-student competition that accompany it) produces undesirable consequences for most students.*
>
> *These undesirable effects include reduction of intrinsic motivation, debilitating evaluation anxiety, ability attributions for success and failure that undermine student effort, lowered self-efficacy for learning in the weaker students, reduced use and effectiveness of feedback to improve learning, and poorer social relationships among the students...*
>
> *Much of the evaluation activity in education might more profitably be directed solely to giving useful feedback to students.'*

For all learners, school students and their teachers, motivation is a key factor in their success. Theories of motivation vary but one common thread is that different people will be motivated by different things: the balance of pressure and support and extrinsic and intrinsic goals will be different from one learner to another. In the Learning School these differences are recognised and respected. Older students in our schools appreciate teachers who can talk to them about such issues, who respect their individuality and regard them as partners in the enterprise of learning. As learners too, teachers need similar respect, recognition as individuals and involvement in school improvement. All teachers are, per se, intelligent, capable, and highly educated, relative to the rest of the population: the Learning School will maximise the potential of its teachers, and benefit from the teachers doing the same with their students.

Key Points

1. **The Learning School builds on the overlap between student assessment, teacher appraisal and school development planning and evaluation.**

2. **Managing this overlap intelligently can save time and energy**

3. **Learning Schools have high expectations of all teachers as well as all students.**

One big question

What would you include in your Portfolio of Achievement?

Further Reading

Patricia Broadfoot (1996): **Education, Assessment and Society,** Open University Press

T. Crooks (1988): **The Impact of Classroom Evaluation Practices on Students,** Review of Educational Research, vol 58, no 4, Winter 1988

T. Crooks, M.Kane and A. Cohen (1996): **Threats to the Valid Use of Assessments,** Assessment in Education, vol 3, no 3, November 1996

Roger Dale (1989): **The State and Education Policy,** Open University Press

M.Fullan (1997): **Emotion and Hope: Constructive Concepts for Complex Times,** ASCD Yearbook, 1997

Caroline Gipps and Gordon Stobart (1993): **Assessment: A Teachers' Guide to the Issues,** Hodder and Stoughton, (2nd Edition)

A.Hargreaves (1994): **Changing Teachers, Changing Times: Teachers' Work and Culture in the Postmodern Age,** Cassell

Tim Horton(ed.) (1990) : **Assessment Debates**

Alfie Kohn (1993): **Punished By Rewards—the Trouble with Gold Stars, Incentive Plans, A's, Praise, and Other Bribes,** Houghton Mifflin

S. Munby, C. Ogilvie and R. Sutton (1987): **INSET and Records of Achievement,** British Journal of In-service education, vol.14, no 1, Winter 1987.

Jean Ruddock, Roland Chaplain and Gwen Wallace (eds)(1996): **School Improvement—What Can Pupils Tell Us?,** David Fulton

R. Sutton (1991): **Assessment, a Framework for Teachers**, Routledge

R. Sutton (1994): **School Self Review**, RS Publications

R. Sutton (1995): **Assessment for Learning**, RS Publications